GREAT GIRLS
IN MICHIGAN
HISTORY

GREAT LAKES BOOKS

A complete listing of the books in this series can
be found online at wsupress.wayne.edu

GREAT GIRLS
IN MICHIGAN
HISTORY

Patricia Majher

Wayne State University Press
Detroit

20 19 18 17 16   6 5 4 3 2

Library of Congress Control Number: 2014953447

ISBN 978-0-8143-4073-8 (paperback)
ISBN 978-0-8143-4074-5 (ebook)

Designed and typeset by Bryce Schimanski
Composed in Joanna MT

To my mother, Irene Vogel Majher,
whose love of reading still inspires me

CONTENTS

INTRODUCTION

What inspires you? Praise from your mom or dad? An A from your favorite teacher? A high five from a friend?

How about a story that focuses on someone your age or a little older who did something really special? Would that inspire you to do something special, too?

In these pages, you'll meet a deep-sea diver and a dancer, an activist and an aviator, a singer and a soldier, a wrestler and a world-class violinist *plus* a dozen other girls from all across Michigan who each did something amazing before she turned twenty.

It wasn't always easy for these girls. Some of them grew up poor. Several lost a parent. One even had to flee in the middle of the night from a heartless slave master. Still, they were able to overcome these obstacles to reach their goals.

And you can, too—even if your goal is just to finish a book report you've been putting off or to go a day without fighting with your brother or sister!

Start small. Then set bigger and bigger goals. And someday you, too, could be a "great girl in Michigan history."

Despite the dangers and the lack of female role models in the field, Fannie Baker fell in love with diving.

FANNIE BAKER

Girl Diver of the Great Lakes
(1884–?)

*Following in her father's footsteps, she dove
to great depths for fun and profit.*

At the beginning of the twentieth century, deepwater diving was a dangerous business. First, there was a heavy suit to put on. The helmet was made of copper and brass. The suit was stitched together from a tough canvas—the same fabric used to make ship sails. And at the bottom of it all were big, clunky boots weighted with lead to keep divers from floating up to the surface before their underwater jobs were done.

Then there was the matter of breathing. The tanks of air that modern divers wear on their backs hadn't been invented yet. So divers had to stay connected by a long hose to an air pump located on a boat. Heaven forbid that something should pinch that hose and restrict the airflow while a diver was down below.

There was one more thing that divers had to watch out for. They called it "the bends." This painful condition, which makes air bubbles form in the lungs, can happen if a diver rises to the surface too rapidly.

All of these dangers were explained to Frances "Fannie" Baker before she took her first dive. And still she said, "Yes!"

Fannie was born in Detroit in 1884 to Harris and Nellie Baker. Mr. Baker was a ship captain with a very special skill: he could dive. Making the most of his talents, he operated a **salvage** business on Lakes Huron and Erie. If a ship was wrecked and its owners wanted it or its cargo brought back up to the surface, he was the man to call.

When Fannie was a little girl, she would watch her father as he donned his work clothes. Though diving suits were heavy and hard to walk around in on land, they were almost weightless underwater. She imagined that, if she could put one on, she would feel as free as a fish in the water. As she grew older, her desire to dive grew stronger, even though there were no other females that she knew of in the business.

When Fannie reached her teens, her father started to invite her on his salvage trips. He didn't have to ask twice; she was thrilled to go. She carefully studied the machinery connected with diving and, in time, learned to command the ship with a confidence well beyond her years.

One day, a big **barge** went down in Lake Huron, and Fannie sailed out to the wreck with her father and his crew. An owner of the barge rode with them and remarked to Fannie how much he would like to recover a diamond ring that he had left in his cabin. "I wonder if your father would get it for me?" he asked.

"I'll get it for you myself!" she cried impulsively, according to an article about her unusual career in a 1905 issue of *Woman's Home Companion* magazine.

She had been dying to make her first **descent**, and here was her opportunity. Her father agreed to let her try and sent along an experienced diver to guide her. Quickly she suited up, walked down the ship's ladder, and disappeared beneath the waves.

The feeling of the cold water caught her by surprise, and she began to breathe in quick, short breaths. Then she closed her eyes for a moment and calmed herself. "I'm where I want to be," she thought. "I'm *who* I want to be."

She slowly descended the fifty feet to the lake bottom and saw the shipwreck looming ahead of her. Following her companion to the wall of the vessel, she climbed up and over it with his help. Just then, she began to feel severe pains in her head and feared that her nose had started to bleed. Unwilling to let that stop her, she reached the cabin of the barge and signaled to the other diver that she wanted to go in first.

In a corner, she saw the nightstand that the owner had described to her and, near it, the small box that held the ring. In her excitement, she stumbled but then regained her balance, finally grasping the box in her gloved hand.

With the pressure of the water closing in on her, she returned to the shipwreck's deck, climbed back over the side, and signaled with a rope that she was ready to be pulled up. Back on the boat, she nearly collapsed from exhaustion. But her father beamed with pride.

As a reward for successfully completing her first dive, Fannie was presented with the diamond ring she had worked so hard to rescue.

This dive marked the beginning of Fannie's fame and fortune. Now she would be able to command between fifty and two-hundred dollars a day as a **salver** like her father.

It was not long after this that she made a gruesome discovery. A schooner went down in Lake Huron, and its crew survived except for one unfortunate seaman. Before the ship was raised for repairs, a dive team was brought together to search for the man's body. One after another, the men returned to Harris Baker's ship empty-handed. Then Fannie stepped forward to take a turn.

Descending into the schooner's cargo area, she swept her flashlight from side to side. And she, too, at first found nothing. Then, as she approached the opening leading back up to the deck, she saw a terrible sight. The ghostly white body of the missing man was bobbing between two deck beams, right over her head. It almost made her scream.

In her work, Fannie sometimes faced real dangers. On one dive, she became tangled up in the wreckage of a sunken boat and had to work furiously for twenty minutes to get her rope free enough to signal for help. Another time, a crew member accidentally knocked her air hose off the pump, bringing her close to suffocating.

But all of these experiences only strengthened Fannie's resolve to be the best diver—male or female—on the Great Lakes. And the best-paid one, too. Within two years of her first descent, she had saved enough money to build a brick mansion all her own on one of the most fashionable streets in Detroit.

In 1904, Fannie Baker made a dive that earned her $5,000 for ten days of work, but it took several years of planning. The ship, the *W. H. Stevens*, left the mining country of the Upper Peninsula with a load of valuable copper bars and headed for Buffalo, New York. All was smooth sailing until the vessel sailed onto Lake Erie. Then the *Stevens* caught fire. The crew escaped on lifeboats in a **gale**, so no one knew exactly where the ship went down.

Salvage companies from Buffalo, Cleveland, and Detroit tried to find it. Months turned into years, and no one turned up a clue.

The mystery of the missing "treasure ship" captivated Fannie. She spent much of her free time studying the details of the fire, the direction in which the wind had been blowing that day, and the depth of the water at the ship's last known location. From these facts, she decided the *Stevens* had gone down near Port Burwell, Ontario.

With that point as a center, she mapped out a square several miles long on each side. "If we drag [nets through] that square," she said, "just as a farmer would plow his field, we will find the copper ship," she told a writer for *Woman's Home Companion*.

The Baker wrecking ship arrived on the scene and spent several days doing just what Fannie suggested. Nearer and nearer it came to the center of the square, until one morning the nets caught on something. A shudder passed through the vessel as it was brought to a stop.

Soundings revealed that the water was eighty feet deep at that point—deep enough to challenge even the most powerful divers. But Fannie insisted that she be lowered to the lake bottom, where she quickly found the remnants of the burned ship. It took some time to bring the copper cargo up to the surface, but the wait was worth it. Everyone on the ship got a little bit richer during that job, thanks to the grit and good instincts of the "girl diver of the Great Lakes."

After She Turned Twenty

Almost nothing is known about Fannie Baker as an adult. It's possible she married and took her husband's name, making it hard to track her through time. Or she might have moved away to try her hand at salvaging along the Canadian side of the Great Lakes or on one of America's other coasts. A newspaper article dated 1904 did trace her to New York City, where she led an unsuccessful attempt to salvage a relative's personal belongings from a wrecked **steamship** named the *General Slocum*.

Wherever she went and whatever she did, she was a pioneer for women in her field—reaching new heights (or, in her case, new depths) in diving.

Sources

Brehm, Victoria. *The Women's Great Lakes Reader*. Tustin, Michigan: Ladyslipper Press, 2000.

Curwood, James Oliver. "The Girl Diver of the Great Lakes." *Woman's Home Companion*, June 1905.

"Girl to Lead Search of Divers for Fortune." *The New York Times*, October 16, 1904.

ONE FINAL FACT

Fannie Baker's diving suit was extremely heavy. The helmet alone weighed fifty pounds on dry land.

Betty Bloomer (*standing, left*) practices in a Bennington College dance class at the age of 19.

BETTY BLOOMER (FORD)

Dancing to Her Own Beat
(1918–2011)

*When you perform a pirouette or try out your best
hip-hop moves, think about Betty Bloomer. She started
her own dance school when she was just a teenager.*

In the first year of her life, Elizabeth Anne "Betty"
Bloomer bounced around a bit. She was born in Chicago and then moved to Denver. By her second birthday,
her family had settled in Grand Rapids, Michigan—the
community she always considered her home.

Betty was, in her own words, "a terrible tomboy." She had
two older brothers and she loved to follow them around, trying to work her way into their football and hockey games—
any activity that involved motion. By the time she turned
eight, her mother had steered her in a direction she thought
was more suitable for a young girl: dance classes. Betty loved
it. "There was no kind of dance that didn't fascinate me," she
told biographer Dan Santow. She started out studying ballet
and dreamed of training at the American Ballet Theatre in

New York City. As the years went by, she couldn't imagine doing anything else with her life.

While attending Central High School, she took a job to help pay for her dance classes. Local department store Herpolsheimer's hired her to model clothing for teenage and young adult women. "I would wander through the store's tearoom wearing an outfit from stock," she explained, "and ladies at the tables would stop me—'just one moment dear, let's look at that'—and I would say '$25.95, third-floor sportswear.'"

At the age of fifteen, she felt confident enough about her talent to rent space in a building and open her own dance **studio**. The Betty Bloomer Dance School charged fifty cents for each child. (She taught some of their mothers the latest dance steps, too!) At the same time, she continued to practice her own skills, saying, "I was looking ahead to a very important career." When Betty was sixteen, her father died from carbon monoxide poisoning while working on the family car in a closed garage. Without Mr. Bloomer's income to rely on, Mrs. Bloomer was pressed to take a job as a real estate agent at a time when few women worked outside the home. Her strength and independence in the face of tragedy greatly impressed Betty, shaping her views on all that women could do.

At about the same time, Betty was invited to attend a performance in Ann Arbor and was introduced to another strong female figure, **modern dance** pioneer Martha Graham. "Once I saw Martha," Betty said, "my whole idea of dance changed." She was in awe of "the freedom of movement

[and] the energy," and she vowed that day to devote herself to this new dance form.

After her high school graduation, Betty spent the summer studying at Bennington College in Vermont, where Graham and other modern dance **choreographers** taught **master classes**. Though Betty danced as much as eight hours a day, she couldn't have been happier—sore feet and all.

After She Turned Twenty

After her second summer away, Betty convinced her mother to let her move to New York City to study with Graham's dance **troupe**. Betty rented an apartment with a friend and found a modeling job to pay for it. Almost every waking moment was spent dancing. Still, though she tried her hardest, she wasn't accepted into Graham's first and best group of dancers.

Betty was disappointed but not discouraged. She was willing to put more time into studying with the troupe. Then a visit from her mother changed her mind.

Mrs. Bloomer missed her daughter very much and asked her to come home for six months. If Betty still wanted to live in New York and be a dancer after that, she promised to accept that decision. Betty, who was a little homesick, said yes.

During that period, she went back to Herpolsheimer's in a new position as the assistant to the fashion coordinator. She also started her own dance troupe as a way to keep her dream alive.

While enjoying time with friends, she met a number of interesting young men and agreed to marry one of them.

But the match, made challenging by her husband's alcoholism, was not a good one. After four years, they divorced.

To heal from this bad experience, she threw herself back into her work. Promoted to the top fashion job, she worked with the clothing buyers, trained models, and put on fashion shows. The hours were long, so when a friend called to fix her up on a date, she said no. The man then got on the phone and talked her into meeting him for just an hour.

This brief date with Gerald "Jerry" Ford—a former football player at the University of Michigan who later went on to law school and served his country with honor during World War II—led to another and another. Six months later, he asked her to marry him. "I took him up on it instantly, before he could change his mind," she joked in her autobiography.

While she planned their October 1948 wedding, he campaigned for a seat in Congress. In November, he won the election, and the young couple headed for Washington, D.C.

That was the beginning of a long period spent in the nation's capital during which Jerry rose to become the leader of his party in the House of Representatives. Because her husband traveled a lot, Betty had to be both mother and father to their children, three boys and a girl. This caused a strain on their marriage.

Betty and Jerry spent long nights talking about this challenge. And just about the time that Jerry agreed to retire from politics, he got a phone call from the White House. The president, Richard Nixon, asked him to become the next vice president of the United States.

Jerry and Betty Ford are joined on a walk around Camp David by their daughter, Susan, and golden retriever, Liberty, in 1976.

The vice president then in office had resigned over a scandal, so someone needed to take his place. Eight months later, a different scandal prompted President Nixon to leave, too. Jerry was there again to lead the country—as the thirty-eighth president—through one of its most trying periods in the twentieth century.

About a month after he became president, Betty was diagnosed with breast cancer. In 1974, people didn't discuss such private topics in public. But the First Lady did, which made millions of women ask their doctors for a test to see if they, too, had this disease.

As Betty realized the power of her position, she began to speak out about issues that interested her. She helped the movement to ratify the **Equal Rights Amendment**, even while protesters marched against her in front of the White House. "I feel women ought to have equal rights, equal **Social Security**, equal opportunities for education, [and] an equal chance to establish credit," she said at the time.

Despite the uproar that some of her opinions caused, she was declared one of *Time* magazine's Women of the Year for 1975.

When the president decided to run for a full term in 1976, she joined his campaign, crisscrossing the country to make speeches. But the constant travel took its toll. She suffered from chronic back pain and didn't get enough sleep, resorting to pain pills and alcohol to help her cope.

Jerry Ford did not win the election. And though *he* moved on to serve on corporate boards and do charity work, *she* felt as though her life had suddenly lost its purpose.

In 1978, her family, very worried about her health, encouraged her to seek medical treatment. Though she resisted at first, she soon came to accept that she couldn't conquer her addictions alone. She spent four weeks recovering in a hospital—a period that she believed saved her life.

As a way of saying thank you for all the support she received, Betty decided to start her own addiction treatment center—one that paid special attention to the needs of women as well as men. The Betty Ford Center opened its doors in Rancho Mirage, California, in 1982. It soon became one of the most respected programs of its kind in the country.

To encourage others to seek help for alcohol and drug problems, she even wrote a book about her experiences titled *Betty: A Glad Awakening.*

In 1991, she was awarded the Presidential Medal of Freedom and, later, the Congressional Gold Medal (which she shared with her husband)—the two highest civilian honors America has to give. But she was modest about her accomplishments. She once explained: "I am an ordinary woman who was called on stage at an extraordinary time. I was no different once I became First Lady than I had been before. But, through an accident of history, I had become interesting to people." Interesting, yes, but helpful, too, in so many ways to so many people.

Sources

Ford, Betty, and Chris Chase. *The Times of My Life*. New York: Harper & Row, 1978.

Gerald R. Ford Presidential Library and Museum. "Betty Ford Biography." Accessed May 8, 2013. www.fordlibrarymuseum.gov/grf/bbfbiop.asp.

National First Ladies Library. "First Lady Biography: Betty Ford." Accessed June 1, 2013. www.firstladies.org/biographies/firstladies.aspx?biography=39.

Santow, Dan. *Encyclopedia of First Ladies: Elizabeth Bloomer Ford*. New York: Children's Press, 2000.

Places to Visit

You can find an exhibit on Betty Bloomer Ford at the Gerald R. Ford Presidential Museum, located at 303 Pearl Street NW in Grand Rapids. For details, go to www.fordlibrarymuseum.gov or call 616–254–0400.

Betty is also honored with a plaque in the Michigan Women's Hall of Fame, 213 West Malcolm X Street, Lansing. For more information, call 517–484–1880 or visit www.michiganwomenshalloffame.org.

ONE FINAL FACT

In 1938, Betty performed at world-famous Carnegie Hall with Martha Graham's dance troupe.

Though she could have continued east on the Underground Railroad, Dorothy Butler settled in Michigan and became a valued member of her community.

DOROTHY BUTLER

Freedom Seeker
(1854–1932)

Against all odds, Dorothy escaped a life of slavery in the South, making her way to a welcoming community in Michigan.

Dorothy Butler was *not* the child of a loving relationship. Her father was the white master of a Kentucky **plantation**. Her mother, Nellie, was one of his black slaves.

Mr. Butler didn't care for Nellie or Dorothy. They were his property, and he gave them no say in how they should be treated. He thought of them as he did a team of horses or oxen—as something to put to work. That could mean anything from laboring in the fields in the hot Southern sun to cooking and cleaning in the master's home. And children worked just as hard as the adults.

The hours were long, and, at the end of the day, Butler's slaves were given nothing but food and shelter for their effort. They were not paid for their work, and they couldn't leave the plantation without permission. They were not free.

Nellie knew what would happen if she and her girls—Dorothy and an older daughter, Sophie—tried to escape from the plantation. They would be hunted like wild animals and forced to return. Punishment, sometimes a whipping, would follow.

As awful as all that sounded, Nellie thought they should try to escape. After all, it was said that some enslaved people had found freedom in the North. Then something happened that gave the little family no choice but to leave. Nellie overheard her master talking about selling Dorothy, then age seven, and fifteen-year-old Sophie at a **slave market** in New Orleans.

Determined to stay together, the trio left Butler's farm during the darkest part of the night. Just as in the book *Uncle Tom's Cabin*, Nellie convinced a man to row them across the Ohio River. From there, they headed north—on foot—through Indiana, following the path of the **Underground Railroad.** They traveled at night to avoid the slave catchers who, by the powers granted in the **Fugitive Slave Act of 1850**, could capture them like criminals.

Along their journey, the Butlers met several "station masters" who gave them food, water, and a place to rest, often hiding them in a barn or a cellar. After 300 miles and many frightening moments, they crossed into Michigan, where they were sent to stay at the home of Dr. Nathan Thomas in the small town of Schoolcraft. Dr. Thomas and his wife were fearless **abolitionists**, risking their lives so that others might enjoy the freedoms they had. It is thought that between 1840 and 1860, the couple helped as many as 1,500 runaway slaves along the road to freedom.

The Butlers stayed for a while at the Thomases' home. Then Dorothy and her mother were invited to live with the family of Delamore Duncan, another abolitionist. Mr. Duncan's sister-in-law, who lived just a few miles west, took in Sophie.

After She Turned Twenty

Although most enslaved people fled to Canada, where slavery was forbidden, the Butlers chose to stay in Michigan, where they were warmly embraced by a tolerant community. In the Duncan home, Dorothy grew to be a happy and healthy adult. For a time, she and her mother lived with Sophie and her husband, who was a soldier in the 1st Michigan Colored Infantry Regiment during the **Civil War.**

Dorothy later worked as a housekeeper and cook, employed—*not* enslaved—in some of the finest homes in Kalamazoo. She was proud to be a free woman.

Sources

Mull, Carol E. *The Underground Railroad in Michigan.* Jefferson, North Carolina: McFarland, 2010.

Southwest Michigan Black Heritage Society, The. "Fugitive Slaves Who Settled in Southwest Michigan: Dorothy

Butler." Accessed August 14, 2013. www.smbhs.org/research.html.

Thomas, Ella. "The Underground Railroad." *Kalamazoo Gazette*, January 4, 1932.

Places to Visit

The Dr. Nathan Thomas House, where Dorothy, her sister, and mother spent their first nights of freedom, is open to the public. It's located at 613 East Cass Street in Schoolcraft. For details, email schoolcrafthistorical@hotmail.com or call 269–679–4304.

ONE FINAL FACT

Dorothy Butler's freedom was finally guaranteed in 1864, when Congress repealed the Fugitive Slave Act.

By the time this photo was taken, Regina Carter had already been playing the violin for six or seven years.

REGINA CARTER

A Musical Marvel
(1966–)

At age two, when most children learn to say no,
Regina said yes to music.

Regina Carter grew up in Detroit, the only girl in a family of three children. When she was two, her older brothers started taking piano lessons. During one of those lessons, she walked over to the piano and played one of their musical pieces by ear. Her parents and the piano teacher were surprised to see such early talent. But they were excited, too, and included Regina in the boys' lessons.

A two-year-old's hands are small, and it was hard for her to stretch her little fingers across the keys. Her piano teacher suggested that she take up the violin instead. When she turned four, her parents enrolled her in special **Suzuki method** classes at the Detroit Community Music School.

A year later, she was offered a chance to play another stringed instrument, but she turned it down. She had fallen in love with the violin—and performing.

Regina spent every Saturday at the music school taking group lessons with her friends. She was trained in **classical music** and, as a "tween," was accomplished enough to play in the youth division of the city orchestra. Through that experience, she was able to take **master classes** from world-famous violinists.

When middle school ended, Regina knew where she wanted to go next: Cass Technical High School. Cass Tech was known for having a strong music program, but students had to apply to get accepted. Regina, with more than ten years of experience, was a shoo-in.

During this time, she not only took violin lessons but viola and oboe, too. She began listening to different types of music and played in a pop music group, but a live performance by a French **jazz** violinist really opened her ears to all that music could be. "Wow, he can **improvise**," she recalled in an interview on the All Things Strings Web site. "He doesn't have to play the same way over and over."

And she tucked that information away to think about later.

At age eighteen, she enrolled in the New England Conservatory of Music in Boston, still focused on classical music and hoping to become a solo performer with a major orchestra, but she didn't feel settled at the school. Something was missing from her life, so she went back to the Detroit area to find it.

Soon she enrolled in the jazz music program at Oakland University in Rochester. A teacher gave her some advice: "Stop listening to violin players; there are too few of them in jazz. Listen and learn from the horn players." He put her in the brass section of the school's big band.

"It was the perfect place for me to be," she told the *Oakland County Prosper*. "And no one thought it odd that I played violin *and* wanted to play jazz music."

When Marcus Belgrave, a famous jazz trumpeter, visited her school, she took master classes from him. He recognized her talent and helped put her in touch with other musicians in the local jazz community.

After She Turned Twenty

After graduation, Regina needed a break from school and lessons and practicing. So she moved to Europe for two years. "When I wanted to play music, I found a band and played with them," she said in her interview with All Things Strings. "Or I taught music. Sometimes, I just goofed off." But Detroit kept calling her back.

In 1987, she returned to Michigan and joined an all-female jazz band called Straight Ahead. She toured and recorded three albums with them before deciding to strike out on her own and move to New York City.

Her first years in that big city were a little lonely. But she met and worked as an **accompanist** for a lot of famous singers, such as Mary J. Blige, Billy Joel, and Dolly Parton. That was great experience.

In 1995, she got a big break when she released her first solo (and self-titled) record. And 2001 was definitely an exciting year. That's when her album *Freefall*, recorded with

Regina returned to her hometown in 2004 to play a violin concerto with the Detroit Symphony Orchestra.

jazz pianist Kenny Barron, was nominated for a **Grammy Award**. Also in 2001, she was invited to play a concert using a violin once owned by the esteemed nineteenth-century musician Niccolò Paganini. She was the first jazz musician *and* the first African American to play this precious instrument, which is considered a national treasure of Italy. Later, she recorded an entire album with it.

Five years after, Regina was awarded a MacArthur **Genius Grant** to support her career. She used the money from the grant to record a new album, *Reverse Thread*, that explored the music of her African ancestors. With that record, she earned a second Grammy nomination.

Regina Carter is still looking for new ways to celebrate the beauty of her instrument. She performs with her own band, which includes a clarinetist, a pianist, a bassist, and a drummer (her husband, Alvester Garnett). She is still connected to Oakland University as an **artist-in-residence**. This time, it is *she* who is teaching the master classes.

Sources

Barbieri, Susan M. "Jazz Violinist Regina Carter: Motor City Maverick." All Things Strings. Accessed June 30, 2013. www.allthingsstrings.com/News/Interviews-Profiles/Jazz-Violinist-Regina-Carter-Motor-City-Maverick.

Niles, Laurie. "Interview with Regina Carter." Violinist. com. Accessed May 30, 2013. www.violinist.com/blog/laurie/20106/11387.

Rupersburg, Nicole. "Regina Carter: World-Renowned Jazz Violinist Cherishes Her Detroit Roots." *Oakland County Prosper*, January 23, 2013. Accessed May 30, 2013. www.oaklandcountyprosper.com/features/reginacarter.aspx.

ONE FINAL FACT

When Regina Carter was very young, she played a tiny violin one-sixteenth the usual size.

Sarah Emma Edmonds's strong face and athletic build helped her pass for a man and serve as a soldier during the Civil War.

SARAH EMMA EDMONDS (SEELYE)

The Secret Soldier
(1841–1898)

*Some girls made baked goods and bandages for soldiers
during the Civil War. But one felt so strongly about
the Union that she enlisted . . . as a man.*

Sarah Emma Edmondson was used to playing the part of a
boy. She was born into a large farming family in New Brunswick, Canada. There was only one son among the children,
and he had epilepsy, a brain disorder that causes seizures. That
meant his sisters had to pitch in to do the work. With all that
had to be done, Emma grew up to be a lean, strong girl. And
she developed some strong opinions along the way.

She didn't get along with her father, who spoke
harshly to his wife and children. He was especially hard
on his son, whom he considered disabled and a disgrace.

When Emma turned fifteen, a neighbor more than
twice her age approached Mr. Edmonson and asked for his

daughter's hand in marriage. Right away her father said yes to the marriage, without asking Emma what she wanted to do.

Emma's mother could see her daughter's discomfort, so she hatched a plan: Emma would secretly leave town with an old friend who was passing through. A few nights later, as the stagecoach pulled away, Emma cut all ties to her family. She even shortened her name to "Edmonds" after that.

The woman who helped her escape operated a hat shop in Moncton, New Brunswick. Emma worked there for the next two years. Then she heard that her father had found her hiding place. Fearing that she'd be forced to finally marry the neighbor, Emma fled again. This time she disguised herself by cutting her hair short and wearing men's clothes. During this period of her life, she called herself Franklin "Frank" Thompson.

At age seventeen, she became a Bible salesman, a job she really enjoyed. But one day, she lost all of her money and all but one of her Bibles. She sold the book for five dollars and used the money to leave the country. "I started for the United States, in mid winter, snow three feet deep," she explained in an 1884 newspaper interview.

Five dollars didn't get her very far. She spent most of her journey walking or begging for rides on passing wagons.

In early 1860, Emma arrived in Hartford, Connecticut, where the company that published the Bibles she had sold was located. To pay for a room at a cheap hotel, she talked someone into buying her pocket watch and used what was left over to replace her travel-tattered clothing. The next day, she stopped by the publishing company and introduced herself as Frank Thompson. Because of her success in selling for them in Canada, they gave her a job and some money to live on.

Within a few months, Emma realized she didn't want to stay in Connecticut. So she set out to travel west, toward new states that were calling for young settlers. She finally stopped moving when she got to Flint, Michigan.

While Emma was in Flint, the **Civil War** broke out. Wanting to show her appreciation for her adopted country, she wondered, "What can I do? What part am I to [play] in this great drama?"

She decided to serve the **Union** as a nurse. (Her years helping her brother had prepared her for this task.) Believing she could get closer to the action as a man, she once again assumed the role of Frank Thompson.

At first, Frank/Emma wasn't allowed to **enlist**; they told her that she was too short. (And her small feet didn't fit the boots every soldier was expected to wear!) But after it became clear that the war wasn't going to be won in a couple of weeks and many more soldiers would be needed, the rules were relaxed. She was **mustered in** on May 25, 1861, joining the 2nd Michigan Infantry **Regiment**.

About a month after the regiment arrived in Washington, D.C., Emma got her first taste of war. During the First Battle of Bull Run in July, she was working in a temporary hospital close to the fighting. The battle swung one way and then the other, until it was certain that the **Confederacy** would win. The Union army then decided to retreat. While tending to the wounded, Emma heard hoofbeats outside. The enemy was getting close, and her patients begged her to leave. In the nick of time, she snuck out a window and escaped on foot, traveling through the woods all night—alone—to catch up to her fellow soldiers.

Later that year, Colonel Orlando Poe asked her to be the regiment's mail carrier. This was an important job that sometimes meant Emma had to cross enemy lines to collect Union soldiers' letters and deliver them to the next carrier.

Because she was on the move so much, no one figured out that young Frank was actually a young woman.

After She Turned Twenty

In 1862, Emma heard that the Union army was looking for someone to become a spy. She decided to volunteer. In her autobiography, *Memoirs of a Soldier, Nurse and Spy*, she wrote that three generals interviewed her. She was tested for her intelligence, character, strength, and shooting accuracy. Once accepted, she had only three days to get ready for her first assignment.

Dressing as a slave, she put on a wig and used chemicals to color her head, face, neck, and hands brown. After entering enemy territory, she met and joined a group of slaves who were carrying breakfast to the soldiers. When that task was done, she was told to help build a barrier wall. She recalled in her autobiography, "I was soon furnished with a pickaxe, shovel, and a monstrous wheelbarrow." All day long, she broke up gravel and shoveled it into a wheelbarrow. It was backbreaking work, but she could see firsthand what the rebels were up to. At her supper break, she drew sketches of their defenses and made a list of the weapons she saw. She then hid both under the inner soles of her shoes. The next day, she traded jobs with a young boy about her size. This move gave her time to talk to **Confederates** as she brought them water to drink.

On her third day in the rebel camp, she was handed a gun and told to fire at any Union soldier who came her way. Left alone to guard a small patch of land, she instead made her way back to the Union line and reported all that she had seen.

This was just one of several missions that Frank/ Emma claimed to have been sent on that year. (Some historians believe she may have embellished the details.)

On May 5, 1862, her regiment came under heavy fire during the Battle of Williamsburg in Virginia. While working with the wounded, she had to put down her medical supplies and pick up a musket to fight off the Confederates. That summer, at the Second Battle of Bull Run, she was thrown from a mule into a ditch. She later recalled, "On crawling out . . . I realized I had sustained severe injuries. I had no use of my left [leg] . . . and the intense pain in my left side, and breast, made me feel sick and faint." She quietly healed from the accident with the help of three soldier friends who brought her food and medicine.

In 1863, Emma developed malaria, a disease of fever and chills, and was expected to report to a doctor for treatment.

But she was afraid that her real identity would be uncovered if she did. So she **deserted** from the army as Frank, spent some time recovering from her illness, and then returned to the war as Emma, a civilian female nurse.

After the war, she went home to New Brunswick, where she rekindled a friendship with a carpenter named Linus Seelye. They wrote letters to each other for a year before deciding to marry. They moved around the American Midwest and spent a couple of years in Charlevoix, Michigan, where Linus had some relatives. Together they had three children and adopted two more.

Though her life was a good one, Emma still suffered pain from her old leg injury and couldn't work. To bring in extra money for her family, she decided to apply for **veterans' benefits**—something unheard of for females.

To give weight to her application, she attended a reunion of her regiment where she revealed that she was a woman. After they got over their surprise, the men gave her letters that vouched for her brave service.

Thanks to their support, Congress voted to give her a monthly pension of $12.

But she still had to take care of the matter of Frank Thompson's desertion from the army. For that, she turned to her old commanding officer, Orlando Poe, for help. His letter may have tipped the scales in her favor. In 1886, she received word that a congressional bill clearing her record had passed and been signed by the president.

RIDING FOR LIFE—Page 217.

Sarah was chosen by General Orlando Poe to deliver important messages behind enemy lines.

By April 1897, Emma had grown quite frail from her injuries and looked much older than her fifty-six years. Still, she traveled from her home in La Porte, Texas, to the big city of Houston to become the only woman accepted as a regular member of the **Grand Army of the Republic** (GAR). Afterward, she called it the greatest honor she had ever received.

She returned to La Porte with a glow that her family had not seen in a long time. But it didn't last long. She struggled through a bout of malaria and then suffered what was probably a stroke. On September 5, 1898, she passed away surrounded by her family. She was buried with military honors in a GAR cemetery in Texas.

In her memoir, Sarah Emma Edmonds Seelye offered this parting comment about her Civil War adventures: "I am naturally fond of adventure, a little ambitious, and a good deal romantic—but patriotism was the true secret of my success."

Sources

Dannett, Sylvia G.L. *She Rode with the Generals.* New York: T. Nelson, 1960.

Edmonds, Sarah Emma. *Memoirs of a Soldier, Nurse, and Spy: A Woman's Adventures in the Union Army.* DeKalb: Northern Illinois University Press, 1999.

Gansler, Laura Leedy. *The Mysterious Private Thompson: The Double Life of Sarah Emma Edmonds, Civil War Soldier.* Lincoln: University of Nebraska Press, 2007.

"Remarkable Career, A." Fort Scott (Kansas) *Monitor,* January 11, 1884.

Places to Visit

Sarah Emma Edmonds (Seelye) is honored with a plaque in the Michigan Women's Hall of Fame, 213 West Malcolm X Street, Lansing. For more information, call 517–484–1880 or visit www.michiganwomenshalloffame.org.

ONE FINAL FACT

As a child, Emma was inspired by a book she read about Fanny Campbell, a real-life female pirate who dressed as a man.

Nancy Harkness first started taking flying lessons at the age of 16.

NANCY HARKNESS (LOVE)

An Adventurous Aviator
(1914–1976)

Nancy Harkness wasn't the first female to earn a pilot's license in the United States . . . just the youngest.

Hannah Lincoln Harkness, later nicknamed "Nancy," was born in 1914 to a wealthy doctor and his wife in the copper-mining community of Houghton, Michigan. Her summers were spent exploring the deep green forests and blue waters of the western Upper Peninsula. But every school year, her parents sent her to a private school in Milton, Massachusetts. They thought she could get a better education there.

At the age of thirteen, Nancy was also encouraged to broaden her horizons by touring Europe with her aunt and cousin in the spring of 1927. While in Paris, France, she had an extraordinary experience: she was at the airport to see the famous American pilot Charles Lindbergh finish the first nonstop, **solo** flight across the Atlantic Ocean. When

Lindbergh got out of his plane, 100,000 people swarmed him. Nancy was part of that excited crowd.

The next year, when Nancy was fourteen, Amelia Earhart became the first woman to cross the Atlantic. And, when Nancy was fifteen, a group of female pilots formed a professional organization called the **Ninety-Nines**.

In 1930, Nancy was horseback riding near her Michigan home when she spotted a small airplane taking off and landing nearby. She soon discovered that a "barnstormer" (stunt pilot) was giving passengers a ride for a penny a pound.

Nancy paid the man and up they went. Then she paid him five dollars, and they took another ride—this one flying out over Portage Lake and Hancock and down the main street of Houghton. The pilot threw in a couple of rolls and loops to thrill her.

And thrill her they did. After a third ride, which cost another five dollars, she was hooked. "You know how it is," she later said in *Michigan History* magazine. "You look at a horse and think, 'I'd like to ride one.' Well, I guess I just looked at that barnstormer's airplane and said to myself, 'I'd like to fly one.'"

At dinner that night, she told her parents that she planned to quit school and learn to fly. Her mother was dismayed by her daughter's demand, but her father came up with a compromise. Nancy could take flying lessons for the rest of the summer but had to return to school in Massachusetts in the fall. As she left for her first lesson, Dr. Harkness advised his daughter to "do it well or not at all."

Nancy was taught by a local pilot who was just two years older than she. "It was a classic example of the blind leading the blind," she noted in an interview in the Texas Woman's University archives. "I was his first student and he was just eighteen!" She soloed for the first time on August 31, and, on September 4, she flew her first dual **cross-country** flight. Less than a week later, she had earned the hours she needed for a private pilot's license.

At age sixteen, she became the youngest woman in America to do so.

When she went back to Milton in September, she could hardly focus on her studies. All she wanted was to do was get up in the air again. To log more hours, she decided to rent a plane and fly a couple of friends to Poughkeepsie, New York. But the problems piled up right away.

First, the plane had a compass she couldn't read. Then, the weather turned bad, and she was forced to fly lower and lower to find her way. She was so low at one point that her oil gauge broke "and smeared black stuff all over the windscreen. I had to hang my head out the open side window [to see]."

Worried that her engine might stop in midair, she made an emergency landing in a farmer's field. Luckily, all on board were safe.

Shortly after that, she had another close call. While flying low over her campus, she almost hit the chapel tower. The school's principal forbade her to go up in the air for the rest of the semester.

In 1931, Nancy enrolled in New York's Vassar College. When not in class, she could be found at the local airport, working toward her **commercial license**. The next year, she had her scariest flight of all.

While riding as a student with a more experienced pilot, Nancy was injured when their plane hit a tree. The aircraft tipped backward after the impact and fell thirty feet onto a stone wall. Dazed from the impact, Nancy unbuckled her seatbelt and fell out, hitting her head on the wall. She probably suffered a concussion and had bad headaches for some time after that. From that day forward, Nancy vowed to always be a careful pilot.

In 1932, at the age of eighteen, she earned her commercial license. Then she set her sights on getting a **transport license**, working on it from Michigan while she recovered from her headaches.

In 1934, just before her twentieth birthday, Nancy Harkness was accepted into the Ninety-Nines.

After She Turned Twenty

The family's finances suffered during the **Great Depression**, a period of great economic distress, forcing Nancy to drop out of college in 1934. To support herself, she served as a **test pilot** and also went to work for a Boston airline founded by a man she later married—Robert Love.

During this time, she tested three-wheeled landing gear, which later became standard on most planes. She also

Nancy and Colonel Robert H. Baker inspect the first group of
Women Airforce Service Pilots in March 1942.

arranged for water towers to be painted with town names
to help pilots find their way around.

When World War II broke out in Europe in 1940,
Nancy offered to pull together a **squadron** of female pilots
who could fly airplanes from their American factories to
military bases, where male pilots would be trained to fly
them. There was a lot of resistance to her idea in the military. Many high-ranking officers believed that female pilots
were bad luck and that they didn't have the nerve to fly
warplanes. But, as the war dragged on and American men
were being shipped overseas by the thousands, the Army
Air Forces had no choice but to agree to her proposal.

At its height, the Women Airforce Service Pilots (WASPs) included more than a thousand female aviators, and Nancy oversaw the entire operation. But she didn't sit behind a desk to do it. She learned to fly every type of military airplane and then trained the women under her command to do the same.

The WASPs successfully delivered more than 12,000 aircraft before being disbanded in December 1944. For her efforts in leading the group, Nancy Harkness Love was awarded the Air Medal. This honor is presented by the military to aviators who excel in leadership and courage during wartime.

After the war, Nancy Love raised three daughters, but she also continued her work as an aviation industry leader and innovator. For instance, she was the first woman with a co-pilot to make a flight around the world. In 1948, after the creation of the Air Force, she was given the rank of lieutenant colonel in the U.S. Air Force Reserves.

One of Nancy's greatest challenges was convincing Congress to allow the WASPs to receive **veterans' benefits**, just like the men who had served during the war. In 1977, that right was finally granted—one year after she passed away. In 2009, the WASPs were honored with the Congressional Gold Medal—the highest civilian honor awarded by the legislative branch of the federal government.

Sources

Douglas, Deborah G. "WASPS of War." *Aviation History*, January 1999.

Draeger, Carey L. "Michigan Profiles: Nancy Harkness Love." *Michigan History*, January/February 1996.

National WASP World War II Museum. "Nancy Love Biography." Accessed August 4, 2013. waspmuseum.org/nancy-love-biography.

Rickman, Sarah Byrn. *Nancy Love and the WASP Ferry Pilots of World War II.* Denton: University of North Texas Press, 2008.

Texas Woman's University Women Airforce Service Pilots Digital Archive. "Nancy Harkness Love Collection." Accessed August 4, 2013. twudigital.contentdm.oclc.org/cdm/landingpage/collection/p214coll2.

Places to Visit

In 1989, Nancy Harkness (Love) was inducted into the Michigan Aviation Hall of Fame, which is located inside the Air Zoo at 6151 Portage Road in Portage. For details, go to www.airzoo.org or call 269–382–6555.

Nancy is also honored with a plaque in the Michigan Women's Hall of Fame, 213 West Malcolm X Street, Lansing. For more information, call 517–484–1880 or visit www.michiganwomenshalloffame.org.

ONE FINAL FACT

Nancy was nicknamed "the flying freshman" when she attended Vassar College.

Julie Harris was a standout actress, even as a child in her Grosse
Pointe school.

JULIE HARRIS

Acting Was Her Life
(1925–2013)

Her first Broadway role was in a play that flopped.
But Julie Harris didn't let that stop her from
chasing her dream.

Julia Ann "Julie" Harris grew up surrounded by wealth in the Grosse Pointe suburbs of Detroit. Her father was a successful stockbroker who could afford to give his only daughter everything she wanted; she grew up in a house so big that she couldn't remember how many rooms were in it. Though Julie enjoyed many privileges, she walked away from them to lead a life that often starts with years of struggle: being an actress.

Julie had a very active imagination as a child, which was sparked by all the movies she saw at her local theater, even seeing one film, *Gone With the Wind*, thirteen times. "That's where I went every weekend," she told a hometown magazine. After hours spent in the darkened room, she would come home and act out all the roles she saw. And she read the biographies of famous actresses, hoping to pick up some acting tips. Julie was also exposed to live performances when her parents took her and her two brothers to see **Broadway** touring companies that visited Detroit.

After years of watching others act, Julie finally got a chance to try out her own skills at the Grosse Pointe Country Day School (now called University Liggett School). Even as a young child, she was something special to watch. At age nine, she **improvised** a dramatic scene that so moved an audience of parents and teachers that they cried.

When she grew older, she was allowed to go to a theater camp in Colorado. The teachers there recognized her talent and pushed the teenager to try out for roles in the works of Shakespeare and Molière, two of the world's greatest playwrights.

Julie spent her last year of high school in New York City at a performing arts school for girls. After that, in 1944, she enrolled in the drama program at Yale University. Within just a few months, she was offered a part in a Broadway play called *It's a Gift*.

"I didn't know what to do," she told a reporter for Senior Women Web. She felt torn between college and what she hoped was the start of her career. So she visited her favorite professor to ask for his advice. "Why did you come here?" he questioned.

"To act," she told him.

"Well, go act!" he said. With his blessing, she accepted the part. She was just nineteen years old at the time.

That part was the first stepping-stone in a career that lasted more than sixty years.

After She Turned Twenty

Even though *It's a Gift* was a comedy, it didn't make the critics laugh. The play closed after only a month and a half—a very short run in the theater business. Julie returned to Yale to finish out the year.

She had bigger roles in six other plays before the decade ended, but most of them also closed within a few weeks. Then, in 1949, she was cast as a motherless tomboy in *The Member of the Wedding.* This was her breakthrough role; she spent almost all of the play onstage, holding her own with her fellow actors and amazing the audience. One critic called her "vibrant [and] full of anguish and elation by turns." Because the play was also a smash hit, she earned a steady paycheck for more than a year.

In 1951, she landed her first starring role as a down-on-her-luck singer in a German nightclub in *I Am a Camera.* For this challenging role, Julie earned her first **Tony Award**.

Both of these plays were made into movies with Julie in the casts. She was nominated for an **Oscar** for the film *The Member of the Wedding*.

Julie appeared in about thirty movies over her lifetime, the most famous being *East of Eden.* In it, she was loved by two brothers, one of them played by a moody young actor named James Dean. It is said that she had a calming influence on him.

She also starred in dozens of television shows, playing historical figures such as France's Saint Joan of Arc and Queen Victoria of Great Britain. It was at this time that Ethel Barrymore, a famous actress of the American theater (and great-aunt to Drew Barrymore), said of Julie, "That girl can do anything."

Julie's modesty made her brush aside the compliment. "An actor *should* be able to play a lot of different colors," she said in the magazine *Heritage.* "That's the challenge and fun of it."

Julie, who was known for her distinctive, lilting voice, won a second Tony in the 1950s and three more in the 1970s. The last of these was for *The Belle of Amherst,* a one-person play about the life of poet Emily Dickinson. In it, she played fifteen different characters! *The Belle of Amherst* ran for more than two years on Broadway, and she also performed it in a touring company, even bringing the company to Detroit. When asked how she coped with doing the same play night after night and keeping it fresh, she responded: "It never gets boring! With each new audience, it's a new experience." Julie shared that bit of advice and many others in a 1971 book called *Julie Harris Talks to Young Actors.*

In 2002, the group that gives out the Tonys presented Julie with a lifetime achievement award. With six Tonys, she became the most honored American theater performer of her time. (Actress Audra McDonald tied her in 2014.)

Most of her roles were dramatic ones. Here she stars opposite Anthony Quinn in the movie *Requiem for a Heavyweight*.

Julie also impressed her peers in television, earning three **Emmys** for her work. For seven years, she co-starred as the mother of a lead character in the nighttime **soap opera** *Knots Landing*. Julie was also a mother in real life. She and her husband, Manning Gurian, were the proud parents of a son, Peter.

Julie continued to work onstage, in the movies, and in TV through the end of the twentieth century. "The roles are still there," she explained to a web interviewer as she grew older. "I just have to be more aggressive about finding them now."

For her extraordinary body of work, Julie was named a **Kennedy Center Honoree**. And, near the end of her life, she was chosen to receive the National Medal of Arts—the highest award given to artists by the U.S. government. President George W. Bush said of her: "It's hard to imagine the American stage without the face, the voice, and the limitless talent of Julie Harris. She has found happiness in her life's work, and we thank her for sharing that happiness with the whole world."

Sources

Harris, Julie, and Barry Tarshis. *Julie Harris Talks to Young Actors*. New York: Lothrop, Lee & Shepard, 1971.

Monaghan, John. "The Fiery Particle from Grosse Pointe." *Heritage*, December 1995.

Mula, Rose Madeline. "Julie Harris: Too Good to Be True?" Senior Women Web. Accessed December 27, 2013. www.seniorwomen.com/articles/rose/articlesRoseIntHarris.html.

Weber, Bruce. "Julie Harris, Celebrated Actress of Range and Intensity, Dies at 87." *The New York Times*, August 26, 2013.

ONE FINAL FACT

In addition to acting in her high school's plays, Julie captained both the fencing and field hockey teams.

Marylou Hernandez (*left*) and her siblings came with their parents from Texas to Michigan every year to pick fruits and vegetables.

MARYLOU HERNANDEZ (OLIVAREZ-MASON)

Yearning to Learn
(1935–)

*Her life in a family of migrant workers kept her from
going to school, so she educated herself.*

During the 1930s and 1940s, Marylou Hernandez and
her family traveled from their home in Texas to work
in the fruit and vegetable fields of Michigan. They were
migrant workers, hired to help plant seeds in early
spring, hoe weeds in the summer, and pick the ripe pro-
duce at the end of the growing season. "We wouldn't get
back [home] until the end of November, first of December," she recalled.

Marylou made her first trip north at the age of three.
Like the adults in her family, she worked six days a week
in all kinds of weather. The farmers who employed them
sometimes provided a barn for them to sleep in. But,

many times, they simply slept in their truck. They didn't make enough money to pay for a campsite or a hotel room.

It was very hard work—all day long, out in the sun. The workers took water with them, but, with no shade, the water became hot. "It was the temperature of soup," Marylou explained in a 2004 oral history interview. "But it kept us alive!" The family also had to take their lunches into the fields, because the farmers wouldn't come back to get them until sundown.

The Hernandez family would travel to wherever the crops were: potatoes in Munger and Edmore, cucumbers in Linwood, peaches in Grand Haven, tomatoes in Blissfield. In Traverse City, the crop was cherries. "You started with the sweet cherries," she explained. "You'd get those done, and then move on to pick the sour cherries."

Marylou dressed in a long-sleeved blouse and pants when she worked in the fields; covering up like that prevented her from getting sunstroke, a medical condition that happens when the body struggles to lower its temperature. On Sundays, though, she'd wear a dress that her mother had made out of cloth flour sacks. Of these dresses she said, "Some had little flowers [printed] on them; some were striped. They were very colorful."

The family's meals were simple; they ate a lot of beans, tortillas, and hot sauce. "If we could afford it," she remembers, "we had hamburger meat and potatoes that we would mix together." Marylou learned how to cook when she was eight so that she could help her mother feed their family at the end of the workday.

For nine years, the Hernandezes lived this life. But all the traveling between states made it difficult for Marylou to get much of an education. She so wanted to learn.

She began to pick up English from talking to the other families she worked beside. Then she taught herself how to read from books provided by the farmers' wives.

Writing was the next skill she tackled. Her father was so proud of an early letter she composed that he carried it around in his wallet for years.

Finally, one of Marylou's uncles stepped in to help. He pointed out to her parents how much she needed a formal education to make her way in the modern world. And he convinced the family to stay in Michigan, offering them a place in his home in the city of Saginaw.

When Marylou was twelve, she began to go to school there. She recalled, "They told me the harder I worked, the faster they would move me up in the grades. There were a couple of teachers who really helped me." Still, it was a struggle. She had a lot of catching up to do; after all, her classmates had started school at age six. She was also told that she couldn't speak Spanish in class. "If you did, they would keep you after school—a whole hour!" she said. Though the punishment seemed unfair, she understood that "it was to get you to learn the language [faster]."

In 1953, when Marylou was eighteen years old, she graduated from high school. The whole family was excited for her. "I was the first to [do that] on both sides," she recalled. Afterward, she wanted to go on to college, but her family needed her to get a job and start earning money.

After She Turned Twenty

Within a year, Marylou met a young man at a dance. After a short courtship, the couple married; they eventually had five children together. "My husband was a good person," she explains. "But we were very young. He was not ready to settle down. He didn't have a steady job, so it was one thing after another."

The challenges became too great to overcome, and the couple got a divorce. Marylou was left to raise her family all by herself.

One of her jobs during this time was in a doctor's office. Always a hard worker, Marylou quickly rose from being the **receptionist** to the office manager. She was great with patients, too; soon, the doctor noticed this and encouraged her to go to nursing school. Though it would be tough juggling work, school, and caring for her kids, Marylou decided to say yes to his idea. At last, she would become a college student.

Because she could only take classes part-time, it took a while to finish her degree, but, in 1969, she did. She also found love again with a man who embraced her and her children.

Marylou put her nursing training to work in a big way in 1986 when she took a job at what is now the Hispanic/Latino

As the head of Michigan's Hispanic/Latino Commission, Marylou had the honor of meeting former president of Mexico Vicente Fox.

Commission of Michigan. There she helped make sure that migrant workers got clean water and proper bathrooms in the field and had access to medical care. She also fought against the use of **pesticides** that could make workers sick.

Over the years, Marylou has been honored many times for her work in improving the well-being of the **Hispanic** community. Today she is the executive director of the commission she joined in the 1980s. But her proudest achievement may be in education; she is the co-founder of a college in Guadalajara, Jalisco, Mexico. Imagine that: a girl who didn't started school until the sixth grade is now helping others reach their goal of graduating from college.

Sources

Ostrander, Stephen Garr, and Martha Aladjem Bloomfield. *The Sweetness of Freedom: Stories of Immigrants*. East Lansing: Michigan State University Press, 2010.

Risper, Rina N. "Our Journeys/Our Stories: Portraits of Latino Achievement." *The New Citizens Press*, February 7, 2014.

Roth, Danielle. Oral History of Marylou Olivarez-Mason conducted for the Michigan Historical Center, May 12, 2004.

ONE FINAL FACT

To remind her of her beginnings, Marylou still keeps the water dipper and sugar beet knife she used as a child in the fields.

A striking beauty in her high school graduation picture, Geraldine Hoff was also a talented artist and musician.

GERALDINE HOFF (DOYLE)

The "We Can Do It!" Girl
(1924–2010)

*A young factory worker became a symbol of strength for
women during World War II and after.*

Geraldine Hoff was born in Inkster, Michigan, one of four
children of an appliance store owner and his wife. The family
was very close; the children often played in the store while
their mother helped their father sell refrigerators and washing
machines. Business was booming, and the money the Hoffs
earned from it provided them with a big house and yard. Life
couldn't have been better for the young family in the 1920s.

Then the **Great Depression** took hold. As the econ-
omy worsened, so did the Hoffs' finances. They eventually
lost their beautiful home *and* the appliance business. When
Mr. Hoff heard that the University of Michigan was hiring
an electrician, he applied for the job and got it. The family
then moved to Ann Arbor.

In the college town, Geraldine grew to become a beautiful child *and* a talented one. She loved acting, art, and music and took cello lessons from an early age. She also wrote poetry—an important skill that helped her cope when her father suddenly died of pneumonia, a lung disorder. Though she was just ten years old at the time, his passing made her feel like her childhood had ended. "We were grown up the next day," she said of the tragedy in an interview for *Michigan History* magazine.

Mrs. Hoff worried about how she would support her family. Even if she could have found a job during the Depression, she didn't know how she'd manage it as she had spinal problems that made standing for long periods of time painful. She ended up renting out rooms in the family's house to make ends meet. Her children earned money from odd jobs they picked up in the neighborhood.

In 1941, another tragedy happened, this one involving the whole country. On December 7, Japanese forces bombed Pearl Harbor, an American naval base in Hawaii. The United States seemed to have no choice but to join with its allies to fight in **World War II**.

In the days that followed the attack, a friend of Geraldine's dropped out of school to **enlist** in the army. Then Geraldine's own sister Virginia joined the Marine Corps Women's Reserve. Those two events helped Geraldine decide that she had to "get busy and do something." She finished high school the following June at the age of seventeen and tried to enlist in the women's branch of the navy, but they wouldn't take her because she wasn't yet eighteen.

Searching for something to do before her birthday, she took a factory job at the American Broach Company in Ann Arbor. They trained her to use a machine that stamped objects out of metal for the war effort.

Soon after she started, a photographer toured the factory and took some pictures of her at work. Geraldine was dressed in men's **coveralls** and wore a **bandanna** on her head to keep her long brown hair out of the machinery. She posed as she was asked to do, then went back to operating her machine.

Geraldine didn't last long on the job, though. She found out that the woman who had used the machine before her had injured a hand while working. That was enough to convince Geraldine, who still played the cello, to quit before she hurt her hands in some way.

By 1942, she found a better job in a local bookstore. That's where she met University of Michigan dental student Leo Doyle. After a yearlong courtship, they were married.

After She Turned Twenty

By 1950, the Doyles had settled in Lansing. There they raised six children. As each child grew older, Geraldine spent more time working in her husband's dental practice. In her spare time, she continued to make music, write poems, and enjoy other artistic hobbies.

Yet all that time Geraldine never knew what happened to the photos she had posed for so many years earlier in a wartime factory. Then she saw one of them in the pages of a 1984 issue of *Modern Maturity* magazine.

Geraldine's photo in a wartime factory was turned into a poster that has motivated millions.

It turned out that the picture had been used to create a poster urging "Rosie the Riveter"—a nickname for the women who took over so many factory jobs when their husbands, sons, and brothers went to war—to work hard on the **home front.** Against a bright yellow background, seventeen-year-old Geraldine is seen flexing her arm muscle and assuring other girls and women that, "We Can Do It!"

Since the 1980s, that image of Geraldine has been used to support many causes relating to **women's rights**. But Geraldine was proudest that the U.S. Postal Service chose to put her strong, confident pose on a postage stamp honoring the sacrifices Americans made during World War II.

After her death in 2010, major newspapers across the country praised her for serving as a wartime inspiration.

Sources

Majher, Patricia. Interview with Stephanie Doyle Gregg, October 19, 2013.

McLellan, Dennis. "Geraldine Hoff Doyle Dies at 86; Inspiration Behind a Famous Wartime Poster." *Los Angeles Times*, December 30, 2010.

Schimpf, Sheila. "Michigan Profiles: Geraldine Hoff Doyle." *Michigan History*, September/October 1994.

ONE FINAL FACT

Though Geraldine Hoff was an athletic girl—enjoying ice-skating and softball among other sports—she wasn't muscular like her image on the "We Can Do It!" poster.

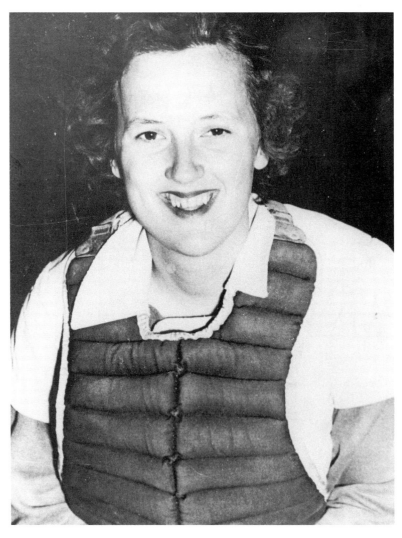

Marilyn Jenkins grew up with the Grand Rapids Chicks but still had to try out for her position as catcher.

MARILYN JENKINS

A Slugger in a Skirt
(1934–)

*She started as a bat girl but worked her way up to
catch for a professional women's baseball team.*

Did you know there was a time when women played professional baseball, just like men? It all started during World War II.

So many players had left the **minor leagues** to fight
in the war that the owners couldn't field full teams. They
were afraid the same might happen with **major league**
players, leading to the collapse of the sport in America.
One owner came up with the idea to replace the men
with teams of female players, and the All-American Girls
Professional Baseball League was born.

Grand Rapids first welcomed a team in 1945. The
Chicks played most of their home games at South High
School, where they drew about 5,000 fans a game. One of
those fans was Marilyn Jenkins. Marilyn loved sports. She
followed local and state teams of all kinds in the Grand

Rapids newspaper. But baseball was her favorite sport. It was her dad's favorite, too. On Sunday afternoons, the two of them would travel across town to see the **Negro League** teams play.

When the Grand Rapids Chicks came to town, Marilyn and her dad attended those games, too, which were played just blocks from their house. One day, he suggested to Marilyn that she walk over and try to get a job with them.

She found a groundskeeper working on the field and asked him if he needed any help. Because she was only eleven at the time, she couldn't operate the lawn mower. So he put her to work picking stones out of the dirt around the bases. Later she picked up trash under the bleachers (and pocketed any nickels and dimes she found).

Before the summer was through, she was asked to be a bat girl. Marilyn couldn't have been more thrilled. "I was just in awe of the players," she remembered in an oral history interview. "They were so nice to me; every one of them was."

Being a bat girl was an important job. Besides picking up the bats after they were used, Marilyn brought balls out to the umpire, shined the players' shoes, and ran errands. All the while, she watched the women as they played and tried to figure out what it took to be a good ballplayer.

She'd been working for two summers for the Chicks when she got terrible news: her father had been diagnosed with leukemia, a bone marrow disease. Despite all medical efforts to save him, he died that fall, leaving Marilyn and her mother to fend for themselves. The Chicks rallied around the Jenkinses, visiting often and sending sympathy cards.

When the next summer rolled around, Marilyn returned to the ball field and to the players who now felt very much like family. As she got older, her job was expanded. Sometimes she'd pitch or catch during **batting practice**. She was learning the basics and getting paid at the same time. And the money helped with her family's finances.

As Marilyn approached the end of her high school years, she began to wonder what she should do with her life. Some of her classmates planned to get married right away. Others wanted to study to be a nurse or a teacher, common jobs for women at that time. Marilyn set her sights on the thing she loved most: playing baseball. She hoped that the Chicks would take her on.

In the spring of 1952, the Chicks held **tryouts.** Though Marilyn worked for the team, she didn't get special treatment. She had to do all the same drills—hitting, throwing, running, catching—as the other girls who wanted to play. But she did have an advantage they didn't: because she was local, the team manager thought she would bring in more fans.

Marilyn ended up making the team but missing the first game of the season. It was a choice of either playing ball or attending her graduation ceremony on that day. Graduation won out.

On the day of her first game, she put on a uniform and was embarrassed. The team required the women to wear skirts—an idea passed down from the men who founded the league—but

Marilyn thought they were too short. "Our legs were bare from mid-thigh to the tops of our socks," she explained to a Grand Valley State University interviewer. "I got some pretty good 'strawberries' [red marks] while wearing them, but it was expected of us." Players were also expected to style their hair and wear full makeup for every game.

The Chicks looked good when they took the field. More importantly, they were a very good team, making the **play-offs** every year. They had lots of talent at every position, so they bounced Marilyn around a bit trying to find the best fit for her. She had a strong throwing arm but not the kind of control you need to be a pitcher. They made her a catcher instead. "I loved it," she said of her assignment. "With every pitch, you're part of the game."

One thing she had to get used to as a catcher was using a catcher's mitt. At that time, they were big, stiff, and thickly padded. If you didn't have the mitt broken in, the ball kept popping out. But Marilyn held on to the ball when it counted, like in the 1953 league championship game that the Chicks won. Marilyn later noted, "That ball is in **Cooperstown** today, right where it should be."

During that championship contest, the Chicks packed 10,000 fans into the stands of South High School's ball field. But the number of fans for regular games got smaller and smaller throughout the league. Why? With the war long over, Americans' attention had turned back toward men's baseball.

The owners of the All-American Girls Professional Baseball League announced plans to shut it down, and some of the young women on the Chicks team were pretty upset by the news. But not Marilyn. Though she loved her sport, she had already begun to think about her future beyond baseball.

After She Turned Twenty

The team was disbanded in 1954. The following year, one of the Chicks was taking classes to become an x-ray technician, and she talked Marilyn into it, too. It took just two years of study to finish the program. Marilyn then landed a good-paying job at a local hospital. She helped the hospital train other technicians, too.

In the 1970s, she switched careers, going to work as a legal assistant for a Grand Rapids lawyer. She also spent several decades working on estate auctions.

In 1982, two hundred former players met in Chicago for the league's first national reunion—and Marilyn was there. The memories shared at one of the later reunions found their way into the script for the big Hollywood movie *A League of Their Own*.

In 2008, Marilyn talked to a filmmaker who was recording the personal experiences of the league's women for Grand Valley State University. When she was asked how playing for the team affected the person she had become, she replied: "It made me competitive but I think in a good way. It also taught me about winning and losing and that

Marilyn (*right*) joined other Chicks at a 2010 event in Grand Rapids that honored their contributions to baseball.

winning isn't everything. . . . I know my dad would have been proud of me, had he lived to see me play."

Marilyn was honored by the Detroit Tigers in 2010 for her contributions to the game. As she told a *Grand Rapids Press* reporter at that time, "[The girls' league] was a heck of a lot of fun."

Sources

Beld, Gordon G. "Sluggers in Skirts." *Michigan History*, March/April 2008.

Boring, Frank. Oral History of Marilyn Jenkins conducted for Grand Valley State University, August 15, 2008.

Zuidema, Michael. "Marilyn Jenkins Among Former Grand Rapids Chicks Set to Attend AAGPBL Reunion in Detroit." *The Grand Rapids Press*, August 3, 2010.

ONE FINAL FACT

As a catcher, Marilyn Jenkins got hit by foul balls all the time. One of the balls dislocated her finger, which is still crooked to this day.

Jane Johnston began to write down the stories and songs of the Ojibwe at an early age.

JANE JOHNSTON (SCHOOLCRAFT)

The First Known
American Indian Writer
(1800–1842)

*Jane introduced America to the power
of her people's words and ways.*

Jane Johnston was born in 1800 in the village of Sault Ste. Marie in what is now Michigan's Upper Peninsula. Though far away from the big cities of the East, the Sault was a vibrant community all its own. A mix of white, Indian, and **Métis** residents helped make it so.

Jane's mother was a member of the Ojibwe tribe and the daughter of a chief. Her Indian name was *Ozhaguscodaywayquay*, but her husband called her Susan. Jane's father, John, was an Irishman who came to the upper Great Lakes in 1790 to make his fortune in the fur trade. Working with Susan and her family to expand his business, John became very successful. The couple, who were much admired in Sault society, built a log cabin that was the largest home in the region.

Jane's Ojibwe name was *Bamewawagezhikaquay*. She was born into two worlds and lived comfortably in both. From her mother, she learned the language of an ancient people and their legends. Jane's father taught her to read and write English using the thousand books in his private collection. Though her brothers and sisters went away to boarding schools to be educated, Jane chose to stay at home and lose herself in that large library.

In 1809, Mr. Johnston took Jane to his native country, Ireland, and to England. What might have been a life-changing trip for her was difficult. She was sick much of the time and missed her mother terribly. Being away made her appreciate her Michigan home all the more.

Three years later, war broke out between the British and the Americans, and John Johnston played a part in it. In 1812, he joined with British forces in capturing a fort on Mackinac Island. Later, when the Americans tried to take it back, he sided with the British once again. He even briefly took command of the fort. But the Americans had their revenge on the Sault Ste. Marie trader. After losing the second battle of Mackinac Island, the soldiers sailed north up the St. Marys River to burn down the Johnston home and business. Fortunately, no one in the family was injured during this devastating experience.

By the end of the war, Jane was fifteen and had turned her attention to writing. She began by putting down on paper the many Ojibwe songs and stories her mother had shared with her over the years. Jane also wrote poems of her own, many of which, like the following excerpt, were inspired by the natural world:

> How all transporting—is the view
> Of rocks and skies and waters blue.

Her most important accomplishment, though, was writing imaginative short stories of her own invention. In one example, "Mishosha," a native magician is punished for his evil ways by being turned into a tree:

> At length the old man reached the brink of the island where the woods are succeeded by a border of smooth sand. But he could go no farther; his legs became stiff and refused motion, and he found himself fixed to the spot. But he still kept stretching out his arms and swinging his body to and fro. Every moment he found the numbness creeping higher. He felt his legs growing downward like roots, the feathers on his head turned to leaves, and in a few seconds he stood a tall and stiff sycamore, leaning toward the water.

These stories—some serious, some humorous, but all of them related to her Ojibwe heritage—made Jane the first known American Indian writer. She was encouraged in this important work by a young man named Henry Rowe Schoolcraft.

After She Turned Twenty

Henry Schoolcraft had been a geologist, someone who studies the Earth and rocks, and an explorer before coming to the Sault in 1822. But his new job in the village was that of an Indian agent who represented the U.S. government in its dealings with the tribes who lived in the area.

Until he could find a place to rent, Henry stayed as a guest in the Johnston home. Jane caught his eye, and he caught hers. But what really made their relationship blossom was a shared love of reading and writing.

Within a year, they married and were living in a wing of the Johnston home that her parents constructed for them. In due time, the Schoolcrafts built their own home nearby and called it Elmwood after the trees that surrounded it.

The early years of their marriage were filled with joy. Their first child, William, was born in 1824, and Jane eagerly accepted her new role as a mother. At about the same time, Henry and Jane started a magazine called *The Literary Voyager*. Each handwritten issue was passed from person to person in the Schoolcrafts' circle of friends. Included in its pages were Jane's poems and short stories—the first time her work was seen outside the family.

In 1827, tragedy struck the young family: Willy died of a breathing disease before turning three. The loss overwhelmed Jane and affected her health, but she worked through her grief by writing some of her most beautiful poetry, such as the following:

May the winds softly blow
O'er thy lone place of rest
And the white drifting snow
Repose light on thy breast.
And when May in her bloom,
A soft **verdure** shall bring
I shall deck thy loved tomb
With the **flow'rets** of Spring.

Later that year, the Schoolcrafts were blessed with the birth of a daughter. They named her Jane and called her Janee. A son, John, followed in 1829.

In the 1830s, Henry's responsibilities increased, and his headquarters was moved to Mackinac Island. Jane and the children accompanied him to his new post. Jane also taught Henry the language and customs of her mother's people, which enabled him to negotiate treaties with the tribe.

While working on the island, Henry began to write down his observations of the tribes he encountered and their stories and legends. Jane was his partner in this project, sharing what she knew about the Ojibwe in the region.

In 1841, Henry lost his job in Michigan for political reasons. Believing it would be easier to find a new job back East, he convinced Jane to leave her **ancestral home** and go with him to New York City. Jane's health was poor, but she agreed to make the trip. When Henry decided to sail to Europe to explore publishing possibilities, she chose to stay behind, making her way to Ontario, Canada, to stay with her sister, Charlotte.

The sisters' three-week visit was a treasured time of reliving childhood memories. Then, on the evening of May 22, 1842, Jane unexpectedly passed away. She was buried in Ancaster, Ontario, far from most who loved her.

Jane Johnston Schoolcraft was not quickly forgotten, though. In the 1850s, her writing gained a new audience when the poet Henry Wadsworth Longfellow drew on her short stories and other sources to create his epic poem *The Song of Hiawatha*. She may even have been the inspiration for the character of Nawadaha, a singer of his people's songs.

> Should you ask where Nawadaha
> Found these songs so wild and wayward,
> Found these legends and traditions,
> I should answer, I should tell you,
> "In the bird's-nests of the forest,
> In the lodges of the beaver,
> In the hoof-prints of the bison,
> In the eyry of the eagle!"

Sources

Brehm, Victoria. *The Women's Great Lakes Reader*. Tustin, Michigan: Ladyslipper Press, 2000.

Mason, Philip P., ed. *Schoolcraft: The Literary Voyager or Muz-zeniegun*. East Lansing: Michigan State University Press, 1962.

Parker, Robert Dale, ed. *The Sound the Stars Make Rushing Through the Sky: The Writings of Jane Johnston Schoolcraft*. Philadelphia: University of Pennsylvania Press, 2008.

Places to Visit

The John Johnston House (where Jane grew up) and Elmwood (the home she shared with Henry Schoolcraft) are open to the public. They are located along Water Street in Sault Ste. Marie. For details, go to www.saulthistoricsites.com or call 906–632–3658.

Jane is also honored with a plaque in the Michigan Women's Hall of Fame, 213 West Malcolm X Street, Lansing. For more information, call 517–484–1880 or visit www.michiganwomenshalloffame.org.

ONE FINAL FACT

Jane's Ojibwe name means "Woman of the Sound the Stars Make Rushing Through the Sky."

As a rising star in the labor movement, Myra Komaroff (*center*) was asked by Governor Frank Murphy to take an important job in state government.

MYRA KOMAROFF (WOLFGANG)

A Fierce Friend of Workers
(1914–1976)

Raised in a family of independent thinkers,
Myra stood up for those who were being put down—
and walked a picket line with them, too.

Mira "Myra" Komaroff was not American by birth, but she very much believed in the country's ideals of liberty and justice for all.

She was born in Montreal, Quebec, to parents who had come to Canada from eastern Europe. Abraham and Ida Komaroff were free thinkers who forged their own path. For instance, though they were Jewish, they chose not to marry in their house of worship. Instead, they were wed in a labor **union** building.

When Myra was about two years old, she and her family moved to Detroit. After working her way through the public school system there, she decided to study interior design at a college in Pennsylvania.

Her father, who sold real estate, did well for himself and his family until the **Great Depression**. Few people could afford to buy property during those difficult years. To make ends meet, the Komaroffs moved into smaller and smaller houses and then into an apartment. It soon became obvious that paying for Myra's schooling was a luxury they couldn't afford. So she was called back to Detroit.

Determined to help her family, Myra visited the office of the local hotel and restaurant employees' union looking for work. When she opened the door, the phones were ringing off the hook. It was just a minute before she started answering them and taking messages. By the end of the day, she had earned herself the job of answering phones and doing clerical work.

Myra came into the labor union world at a time of great change. New laws were making it easier for unions to organize and work with **management** for the benefit of their members. And a recent strike against General Motors in Flint had ended in the workers' favor. Myra was very excited about her new position. She soon found herself working not only inside the office but outside it, too—helping waiters, waitresses, cooks, and hotel workers settle complaints with their bosses.

Sometimes those complaints were widespread. For example, *all* of the **laborers** of a business might be working too many hours for too little money. That was the case in 1934 at Charlie Shannon's Bar. And when the staff decided to walk off their jobs and **picket** the place, Myra was right there with them.

The owner called the police, who came and carted everyone off to jail. Myra and the workers stood strong, though; after being released, they went right back to the business and got arrested again.

Seeing how serious his employees were about being treated fairly (and worried that he might lose some business), the bar owner agreed to their demands.

This was Myra's first victory as a union **activist**.

After She Turned Twenty

In the fall of that year, Myra was asked to join the executive board of her local union—a big honor for a twenty-year-old.

Myra had many strengths as an activist. She was confident, a powerful speaker, and totally committed to her cause. In 1937, she organized a **sit-down strike** of lunch counter workers at a Woolworth's department store. The strike, which drew national attention, lasted eight days, and she spent every moment of it inside the store making sure the women knew that their union supported them. She later brought 7,000 hotel workers into the union by gaining better working conditions for them.

In 1936, Michigan Governor Frank Murphy appointed Myra to a government position that enabled her to help the unemployed. It was an honor to be asked to do this, and it paid more than her regular job. She took the position but still remained a union board member.

Myra (*left*) was one of the "founding mothers" of the Coalition of Labor Union Women.

In 1939, she married a lawyer named Moe Wolfgang. He was also sympathetic to unions and often gave her free legal advice. Most importantly, he valued her job as much as his own. When their two children came along, he spent as much time raising them as Myra did.

Their equal relationship helped Myra reach new heights in her career. With Moe's income to fall back on, she quit her state job and returned to the local union office that she loved. She was also free to travel outside of Michigan. At one point, she helped **negotiate** a union **contract** for employees in the hotels of Miami Beach, Florida.

Myra was widely known for making sure that women in the restaurant and hotel business were treated fairly, with rules in place to limit the amount of weight they were required to lift and the number of hours they had to work. She also fought against racial discrimination and marched for civil rights in Selma, Alabama.

Around 1960, Myra began to wonder why Michigan did not have a **minimum wage** law. It took four years and many trips to Lansing to persuade legislators of the need for this change. But, finally, they voted to require every employer to pay every employee at least $1 an hour.

Not one to rest on her successes, she worked to have the minimum wage raised even higher. She organized a "sleep-in" at the capitol and joined seventy-five protesters in spending the night in sleeping bags in the senate chambers. The protesters left peacefully the next morning, but state government got the message: Myra Wolfgang wouldn't stop until those with the lowest wages were paid more. For her decades of hard work on this issue and many others, Myra was named a vice president of her union.

Near the end of her career, she began to talk with others in the labor movement about how they could help more women become leaders in their unions. In 1974, she chaired the very first meeting of the Coalition of Labor Union Women (CLUW), where more than 3,000 women gathered from eighty-two unions across the country. CLUW is still operating today as a strong organization fighting for the rights of unionized female workers.

Clearly, Myra Wolfgang was known for her fighting spirit, too. In *Michigan Jewish History* magazine, she was quoted as saying, "I don't look for trouble. But, by God, I don't run away from it."

Sources

Pitrone, Jean Maddern. *Myra: The Life and Times of Myra Wolfgang, Trade-Union Leader.* Wyandotte, Michigan: Calibre Books, 1980.

Ware, Susan, ed. *Notable American Women: A Biographical Dictionary Completing the Twentieth Century.* Boston: Harvard University Press, 2004.

Wolfgang, Martha, and Laura Green. "Labor's Champion: Myra Wolfgang." *Michigan Jewish History*, Fall 2010.

ONE FINAL FACT

Myra's union friends gave her the nickname "La Pasionaria," the passionflower, for her commitment to their cause.

Even at the age of four, Julie Krone led her pony with authority.

JULIE KRONE

Born to Race
(1963–)

*Julie Krone was winning horse races before
most girls her age could drive a car.*

Julieann "Julie" Krone rode her first horse when she was only
two years old. She was sitting on a palomino her mother was
trying to sell, helping to show how gentle the horse was. Suddenly, the mare trotted off with the toddler on its back. When
it stopped, Julie reached down and grabbed the reins. She
led the horse as it turned around and came back to where it
started. That's all it took to make Julie fall in love with these
big, beautiful animals.

She grew up on a farm in Eau Claire, which is in the
southwest corner of Michigan. Her parents both encouraged her to ride. Her mother was a horse trainer and riding teacher, so Julie's lessons were free. Before she was old
enough to go to school, she knew how to bridle and saddle
a horse and how to control it with her hands, legs, and

feet. Her father was an art teacher and photographer who eagerly grabbed the camera to record his daughter in action.

In childhood, Julie rode a pony named Filly. Every horse has its own personality, and Filly had a bit of mischief in her. When Julie tried to put a bridle on her, Filly would resist. If Julie tied her to a fence, the pony would chew through the rope to get loose. And when Julie rode her, Filly would sometimes buck her off and run away. "There'd I'd be," she said in her autobiography, "miles from home."

It was hard for Julie's mom to watch these struggles. At one point, she thought about selling the pony and finding another that was better suited to her daughter. But Julie refused to let Filly go and promised to work twice as hard to train her. Julie didn't know it at the time, but learning how to work with Filly's sometimes nasty nature would help her in her future career.

When Julie was just five years old, she began to compete in riding contests at the county fair. In her very first contest, she rode against girls who were as much as fifteen years older, and Julie won! Her early training paid off.

She joined the local **4-H** club to meet other horse-loving kids. They called themselves the Road Runners because they spent their summer days riding their ponies up and down the country roads. But they also put many hours into learning how to care for their animals.

Through her grade school years, Julie kept competing in riding contests. And she kept on bringing home blue ribbons. As a teenager, her winning streak continued.

Unfortunately, Julie didn't have the same kind of success in school, and it really showed when she started high school. She did well in her art classes but not in anything that involved reading or math. "Teachers would tell me I was a horrible speller, or a slow learner, or a problem student," she remembered. It wasn't until Julie grew older that she learned she had dyslexia, a disorder that can make reading, writing, or working with numbers difficult.

She began to doubt herself and wonder what she could become if school was going to be so hard. At the age of fifteen, she found her answer. Julie watched the world-famous Kentucky Derby horse race on television that year and was so impressed by the winning **jockey**, Steve Cauthen, that she decided to become one, too.

The next day, she went to a bookstore and bought a book about Cauthen. Then she read one about Bill Shoemaker, the "winningest" jockey in the world. Later she bought an encyclopedia about **thoroughbreds**.

During spring break of her sixteenth year, Julie and her mother left their Michigan home and drove to Churchill Downs, the home of the Kentucky Derby. Both of them found short-term jobs as **hot-walkers**. It wasn't a glamorous job, but Julie loved it and worked hard to show it. The people at the racetrack noticed the spunky teenager. By the end of the week, one trainer offered her a summer job.

Julie could hardly wait to return to Kentucky, making the last few weeks of the school year almost unbearable. The night before her mother drove her back, the two saddled their horses and went for a midnight ride. They sang the song "Don't Fence Me In" at the tops of their lungs. Julie felt like she was being set free.

As the new kid on the block at Churchill Downs, she had to put up with some teasing from the other stable hands. One asked her to fetch him a bucket of steam. (A joke.) Another called for a "saddle stretcher," a task that took her several hours of searching to figure out. (It was another joke.) But Julie soon settled into the routine of track life. Within three weeks, she was promoted to the job of a groom, a person in charge of cleaning and feeding the animals.

Dying to ride one of the thoroughbreds, she almost jumped for joy when the trainer asked her to **breeze** his horse. Before the summer was over, she was even allowed to ride the lead pony that escorts and calms thoroughbreds before their races.

Back at school for her junior year, Julie continued to struggle in her classes and even started to skip school. Her desire to become a jockey was beginning to overwhelm her.

Her mother did the only thing she could think of to help: at the end of the school year, she sent Julie to live with a friend whose husband raced **quarter horses**. The couple lived an hour from Julie's Eau Claire home and right next to a Michigan racetrack.

Julie spent the summer of 1980 racing horses in Michigan, Ohio, and Illinois, building a solid reputation as a rider. At one track, the announcer said of her: "There's Julie

Krone, one of the best little jockeys, male or female, we've had at the fair in ages."

Julie returned to Eau Claire for her senior year of high school but dropped out in December—against her father's wishes—to move in with her grandparents in Tampa, Florida, to pursue her dream. Her mother drove her down south and stayed a week to make sure that Julie was settled. In that time, Julie met a trainer who was willing to help her become an **apprentice jockey** and earn her license to ride. (The process was similar to getting a license to drive.)

Julie took to her new job quite well. In her fifteen years of riding, she'd met easy horses and hard ones and had learned how to get the most out of every one of them. She competed in her first race in January 1981, on a horse called Tiny Star, and was disappointed to come in second. But her trainer saw potential. He told everyone who would listen that Julie would be "a very famous jockey someday, and her picture is going to be on the front of magazines."

He even talked about her with his competition. One of those men agreed to let Julie ride a big chestnut thoroughbred named Lord Farkle. On February 12, 1981, she paid him back for his kindness by winning a race at Tampa Bay Downs. "As we thundered down the stretch I kept thinking, 'When are all the horses going to pass me?'" No one did.

Julie was just eighteen years old.

When an apprentice jockey wins her first race, all the other jockeys pile on her and cover her with a mixture made of peanut butter, black shoe polish, baby powder, and shaving cream. Despite the sticky mess that Julie endured that day, nothing could take the smile off her face. Her dream of riding racehorses—and winning—had come true.

After She Turned Twenty

In the 1980s, Julie Krone rode hard and well, winning 1,898 races and earning a spot on the cover of *Sports Illustrated* magazine. In 1993, she became the first woman to win a **Triple Crown** event: the Belmont Stakes. That same year, the sports TV network ESPN named her the year's top female athlete. She felt like she was on top of the world.

But horse racing is a dangerous sport. And Julie was soon to find out just how dangerous it could be.

On August 30, 1993, she was riding Seattle Way at the Saratoga Raceway in New York when a second horse veered into their path. Seattle Way's front hooves became tangled in the other horse's heels, and Julie was thrown off. She landed awkwardly on her feet, then bounced into a sitting position. Another horse—all 1,200 pounds of him—ran directly into her, kicking her in the chest. If she hadn't been wearing a protective vest, the kick might have killed her. Even so, she suffered a bruised heart and a shattered ankle.

Surgeons used two steel plates and fourteen screws to repair her ankle. Months of physical therapy followed. During that time, she worried how she could make it back to the sport she loved. "What if I've lost my talent?" she thought. "What if I'm not the rider I was before?"

Though officially retired, Julie saddled up again for a race held in Doncaster, England in 2011.

In April 1994, Julie drove from her home in New Jersey to Belmont Park, where she'd won the Triple Crown race. She was determined to find out if there was still a place for her in racing. She galloped a couple of horses for a bit, but when she stopped riding, the exhaustion hit. She knew then that she still had a way to go to get back into shape.

In late May, she was asked to ride in her first race since the accident. "Part of me sang at the thought of riding racehorses again," she said, "while another part made my legs shake."

But the moment she mounted the horse and headed for the track, she stopped worrying. It felt right to be back in the saddle again.

Though Julie didn't win that day, she did the next. And all the while her family, friends, and fans cheered her on.

Over the next two years, Julie continued her winning ways. Then she suffered another fall that broke both of her hands. Though she was back in the saddle in six weeks, something had changed inside of her. She was overwhelmed with flashbacks of her accident and became afraid to take risks. Trainers made the problem worse by pulling her off her favorite mounts. Other jockeys called her "chicken" and told her to quit. "My heart was gone, and I [couldn't] ride like that," she told a *New York Times* reporter.

Julie's healing process began with a conversation with a racing fan who was also a psychiatrist. He diagnosed her as having **post-traumatic stress disorder** as a result of her accidents and recommended talk therapy and medication to calm her anxieties.

With these treatments, she was able to return to the sport she loved. But she didn't win as much as she had early in her career. This prompted her to retire from jockeying in 1999.

Not one to sit on the sidelines, Julie took a job as a horse racing analyst for a TV network. She also earned her high school diploma and took college courses in psychology. Then, in 2000, she was recognized for her amazing career by being inducted into the National Museum of Racing and Hall of Fame—the first woman to win such an honor.

Julie has come out of retirement to race on occasion. In August 2003, she became the first female jockey to win a race with a prize of a million dollars.

In 2005, she brought home a prize much greater than that when she and her husband, Jay Hovdey, welcomed their baby girl, Lorelei.

Sources

Krone, Julie, and Nancy Ann Richardson. *Riding for My Life*. Boston: Little, Brown and Company, 1995.

Lipsyte, Robert. "Julie Krone's Race Against Depression." *The New York Times*, May 21, 2000.

Miller, Mark. "I Wanted to Be a Jockey." Jockeysite.com. Accessed January 1, 2013. www.jockeysite.com/stories/juliekrone.htm.

Stout, Glenn. *Yes She Can! Women Sports Pioneers*. Boston: HMH Books for Young Readers, 2011.

Places to Visit

Julie is honored with a plaque in the Michigan Women's Hall of Fame, 213 West Malcolm X Street, Lansing. For more information, call 517–484–1880 or go online to www.michiganwomenshalloffame.org.

ONE FINAL FACT

Julie made a living out of being only four feet, ten-and-a-half inches tall—a perfect height for a jockey.

Joan Leslie's dream role was acting (and dancing) opposite Fred Astaire in *The Sky's the Limit*. She was eighteen at the time.

JOAN LESLIE (CALDWELL)

Silver Screen Star
(1925–)

*Joan Leslie went from singing on the local stage
at age three to acting in Hollywood movies by the
time she was eleven.*

Joan Agnes Theresa Sadie Brodel was just a toddler when
she joined her two sisters, Betty and Mary, in a singing-
and-dancing act in the late 1920s.

They performed mostly at church socials and fund-raising
events in their hometown of Highland Park, Michigan. It was
really a family affair with their father, Frederick, driving the
girls to their performances and their mother, Agnes, serving
as their **agent** and **accompanist**. Agnes also made sure that
their performances didn't get in the way of doing their home-
work. The girls attended St. Benedict's Catholic School.

As the trio grew older, they acquired more musical
skills. Joan learned to play the accordion while Betty and
Mary picked up the banjo and saxophone.

The two older girls would start the performance. Then young Joan would come onstage and do a musical number of her own as well as impressions of movie stars of the day. She would then finish the performance with a crowd-pleasing dance number. "I killed 'em," she remembered with a laugh to a reporter for the Western Clippings Web site.

In 1929, when Joan was just four, the stock market collapsed. The **Great Depression** threw millions of people out of work, including Mr. Brodel, who had held a day job as a bank teller. That meant the family had to depend on the money earned by the girls' performances to make ends meet.

The Brodels may have been struggling, but they were hopeful, too. Frederick and Agnes were convinced that their girls had something special to offer. So they packed up the family and drove west to Hollywood, California, the home of the movie-making industry.

Joan, then eleven years old, passed a **screen test** and was offered a **contract** by MGM Studios. Her first role was a **bit part** in *Camille*—a promising start in a movie that was a blockbuster hit of its era. During this period, Joan attended the studio school with other child actors. But her time in Hollywood was brief; MGM decided not to renew her contract, and the Brodels drove back to the Midwest. Then her sister Mary was offered a contract by Universal Studios, so it was back to California for the family.

While Mary was working at Universal, Joan spent the next five years playing small parts. In 1940, one of those led to a Warner Brothers' contract. But the studio had one request: she would have to change her last name. From that point forward, she was known as Joan Leslie.

Though not yet sixteen, Joan looked older than her age. This enabled the studio to cast her in adult roles. In her first movie for Warner, she co-starred in *High Sierra* with Humphrey Bogart—the biggest movie star of the day. In between scenes, she was tutored on the set. "That was kind of hard on my leading men," she said in an interview with film scholar Bill Ruehlmann. "I would be doing a romantic scene, and the director would say, 'Okay, print that. Now, Joan, go to school!'"

She made five more films in 1941, including *Sergeant York* with another big Hollywood star, Gary Cooper. She'd grown up watching Cooper and didn't know how to behave around the famous and much older actor. But their first meeting set the tone: "When I looked up at Gary, he just twinkled down at me and said, 'How do, Miss Gracie?' That was my character name. He set me at my ease with that."

After the studio bosses saw how well she did in *Sergeant York*, they cast her as Mary, the wife of composer George M. Cohan, in *Yankee Doodle Dandy*. She loved working with her co-star, James Cagney: "He was an absolute joy— an inventive, creative, sincere actor. He just gave so much and made me better than I was."

As much as she enjoyed working with these leading men, what Joan really wanted to do was star with dancer Fred Astaire. "When I came to Hollywood, I wrote Mr. Astaire a letter saying 'I'm paying daily visits to the wishing well, hoping I can sometime play opposite you.'" When she was eighteen, she got her wish: Astaire asked her to co-star with him in *The Sky's the Limit*. She was the youngest female to ever dance with him in a movie.

During World War II, Joan visited army camps to boost the spirits of men who were training to go overseas. She also starred in nine more movies, many with a patriotic theme.

She left her teens just as the war was ending.

After She Turned Twenty

Shortly after her twenty-first birthday, Joan did something very gutsy for the time: she sued her studio to get out of her contract. "The movie industry was changing and television was coming in," she explained. "The studios were playing it safe and making cheaper pictures. I didn't like that, and I wanted to have a say in my roles."

She thought she might have a case, because she was a **minor** when she signed the contract. But, in the end, the court sided with Warner Brothers. Despite the fact that they won, the studio executives were angry with Joan and ended up dropping her from the company. They asked other studios not to hire her, either—a problem that lasted for more than a year. Finally, she was able to get work again.

At the end of the 1940s, Joan Leslie's life moved in a different direction. She met a man she wanted to spend her life with: Dr. William Caldwell, a Los Angeles doctor. After

Joan works hard for charitable causes. She is shown here at a fundraising event in 2006.

marrying him and giving birth to twin daughters, Patrice and Ellen, Joan retired from performing for a while.

As her girls grew older, she found time to fit a movie role or two into her schedule. She also took on several TV roles, making guest appearances in such shows as *Murder, She Wrote* and *Charlie's Angels*. Altogether, she appeared in forty-six movies and twenty-five TV shows.

With fan support, she was honored with a star on the Hollywood Walk of Fame. She passes her time today with community work, including serving on the board of a Los Angeles-based charity that supports pregnant women and young mothers and their children.

Sources

Fitzgerald, Mike. "An Interview with Joan Leslie." Western Clippings. Accessed August 5, 2013. www.westernclippings.com/interview/joanleslie_interview.shtml.

Hollywood Walk of Fame. "Joan Leslie." Accessed August 5, 2013. www.walkoffame.com/joan-leslie.

Internet Movie Database. "Joan Leslie." Accessed August 6, 2013. www.imdb.com/name/nm0504125/?ref_=tt_cl_t2.

Ruehlmann, Bill. "Joan Leslie Interview." Joanleslie.com. Accessed December 8, 2013. www.joanleslie.com/Interview01.html.

ONE FINAL FACT

In the movie *This Is the Army*, Joan co-starred with future president Ronald Reagan.

Maebelle Mason proudly wore the medals she earned for lifesaving in this portrait.

MAEBELLE MASON (CONNELL)

The Littlest Lifesaver
(1875–?)

Maebelle Mason was small for her age. But that didn't stop her from trying to save a man from drowning in the fast-paced Detroit River.

Maebelle Mason grew up surrounded by water. She and her parents, Orlo and Belle, lived on an island in the Detroit River, which flows between Michigan and Ontario, Canada.

The island—called Mamajuda—was just a few acres in size. But its importance was great, for on the island sat a lighthouse built by the U.S. government to warn ship captains of a dangerous hazard in the water nearby.

Maebelle Mason spent most of her childhood on Mamajuda Island. She moved there in 1885, when she was nine; that's when her father was named the keeper of the lighthouse. Being the keeper was a critical job. Many ships sailed the Detroit River on their way to and from the port cities of the upper Great Lakes. The last thing the captains needed was to run their ships into the shifting sands of the waterway and risk damage . . . or worse. Orlo made sure that they all passed by the island safely.

Working at a lighthouse had its challenges. The keeper was responsible for making sure that a series of oil lamps stayed lit at night at the top of the tower. On a calm evening, that meant waking at least once to make sure the lamps still had oil. In a storm, a keeper would stay awake all night to keep the flame from blowing out.

In the morning, another set of duties waited. A keeper had to clean the oil smoke from the windows around the lamp, then do any cleaning or repair work needed in the tower or in the keeper's cottage. Keeping a record of such things as ship traffic in the river and the weather was another responsibility.

Orlo Mason had no assistant keeper, so he relied on his wife to help him with the daily work. As Maebelle grew older, she learned how to help, too, despite the fact that she was small for her age. Typically, a child's chore list would include polishing the brass on the keeper's tools and the tower's equipment.

The government gave the Masons all that they needed to run the lighthouse, such as oil for the lamp and firewood for the stoves, but they had to buy their own food and clothing and just about everything else. All of this could be purchased in the nearest town, which was Wyandotte, Michigan.

On a clear, cool day in May 1890, Orlo Mason set out for Wyandotte in the lighthouse boat with a grocery list in his hand. He had left his wife and daughter behind, but that was not unusual. He trusted them to take care of the tower while he was gone.

Not long after Orlo sailed away upstream, a man came downstream in a rowboat. He'd been rowing for some time and began to get tired. Thinking he might get a free tow, he tossed a rope to a nearby **steamship**, but the rope fell short. The rowboat capsized in the steamer's **wake**, tossing the man into the river, which was still icy cold from the spring thaw.

The captain of the steamship saw what had happened and, as he passed the lighthouse, called out to see if someone could rescue the soaking-wet sailor. Belle and Maebelle heard the call and ran to their spare boat as fast as they could.

The boat was a **punt**, which is more suited for skimming along the shoreline than plunging into the river's strong current. But it was all the Masons had.

For a second, Belle hesitated to attempt a rescue, so young Maebelle made a decision to take charge. She jumped into the boat, grabbed the oars, and started rowing away.

After a mile of backbreaking work, she found the man, who was exhausted from trying to stay afloat. Despite the fact that he outweighed her, she was able to pull him into her boat and also tie up his boat alongside. She then started to row herself and her shivering passenger back to Mamajuda.

When they arrived at the island, the man was so thankful to be saved that he cried. And Belle couldn't help but be impressed by her brave, lifesaving daughter.

News of the sailor's rescue spread fast along the river, from city to city and from ship to ship. Soon everyone in the area was aware of Maebelle's act of courage. Word also reached the government in Washington, D.C. The Department of the Treasury, which was in charge of the U.S. Lighthouse Service, gave Maebelle the Silver Lifesaving Medal for her efforts.

It was rare that a child should receive such an honor, let alone a girl. (The accomplishments of females were not often recognized during this era.) Maebelle received her medal at the Cadillac Hotel in downtown Detroit in front of the national meeting of the **Grand Army of the Republic**. But that wasn't the only honor she earned. The **Shipmasters Association** was so impressed by her bravery that they gave her a double medal made of gold.

To celebrate her achievement, Maebelle's parents paid for her to pose for a photograph wearing her "hardware." The medals were as large as those her father had earned in the **Civil War**.

It took a little time for the excitement to die down, but Maebelle's life at the lighthouse did return to normal. She continued to be a great help around the lighthouse and stayed with her parents on the island until she got married.

Something did change, though, in the years between the rescue and her wedding . . . something very special. And it made Maebelle feel very good. Whenever a steamship flying the flag of the Shipmasters Association passed the island, its captain would blow his horn out of respect for the great girl who risked her life to row to the rescue.

After She Turned Twenty

Not long after the rescue, Maebelle settled into a life of marriage and motherhood. On June 21, 1892, she and James Connell, a machinery engineer, were wed. In 1896, she gave birth to a son whom she named Orlo James in honor of her father. Five years later, a daughter, Corrine, was born.

Sources

Biggs, Jerry. "Mission to Mamajuda." *Lighthouse Digest*, October 2000.

Druett, Joan. *She Captains: Heroines and Hellions of the Sea.* New York: Simon & Schuster, 2000.

Mansfield, J. B., ed. *History of the Great Lakes, Volume II.* Chicago: J. H. Beers & Company, 1899.

ONE FINAL FACT

Maebelle Mason is one of only 1,900 people to have received the Silver Lifesaving Medal since the first one was awarded in 1874.

Ella and her sister decorated the graves of both Confederate and
Union soldiers.

ELLA MAY (WILLSON)

A Petite Patriot
(1854?–1901)

Her simple gesture of laying flowers
on a grave turned into a national holiday
that we still celebrate today.

It was 1862, the second year of the **Civil War**, and Ella May was right in the thick of it. The eight-year-old girl was moving through enemy territory with Michigan's 2nd Infantry **Regiment**.

What was Ella May doing so close to the fighting? Her father, Franklin, was the regiment's **chaplain**. And, as an officer, he was allowed to bring his family along.

Ella, her older sister, Josephine, and their mother, Maria, had followed the chaplain from Kalamazoo, Michigan, to Virginia. In Alexandria, Maria—who served as an unofficial nurse to the regiment—smuggled badly wounded **Union** soldiers into the **Confederate** city's hospital so that they might receive better treatment. For her efforts, she was called "an angel of mercy from God." She set a good example of kindness for her daughters.

On April 13, 1862, the one-year anniversary of the start of the war, the Mays were staying in Arlington Heights. Ella and Josephine walked around the grounds of a beautiful estate gathering wildflowers. With their hands full of the blossoms, they came upon a grave—a rough mound of dirt under which lay a soldier who had died in a battle nearby. Without a moment's hesitation, the girls dropped down on their knees to lay their flowers on top of it to honor the brave man who had given his life to save the Union.

On their way home, they decided to pick more flowers and put them on all the graves they could find. When they shared their plan with their mother, she was touched by their thoughtfulness and decided to join them in their commemoration of the dead. The next day, the May women and a friend covered thirteen graves—Union *and* Confederate—with their floral gifts.

In 1863, on that same April day, they repeated their efforts of the previous year and the year after that, too, visiting Fredericksburg and other battlegrounds in the state. People began to talk about what the girls were doing, and the idea of honoring fallen soldiers soon spread to other states. There was no shortage of graves to tend; one out of every four men who went to war never made it home.

The girls didn't get a chance to place flowers on the fourth anniversary of the war's beginning. That's because Robert E. Lee, the general in charge of the Confederate forces, had surrendered his troops several days before. Michigan's 2nd Infantry Regiment was there to see it. A cheer went up from the battle-weary soldiers. They were finally going home.

By the summer of 1865, the regiment was **mustered out** of service, and the May family had returned to Kalamazoo. Franklin May went back to his work as a minister, and Maria and their daughters settled into the lives they had led before the war took them all away.

As the years passed, Ella finished school, and Josephine developed her homemaking skills. Back East, where their father had served, the girls' practice of decorating graves had continued on despite their absence.

In 1868, General John Logan, who was in charge of the **Grand Army of the Republic** (GAR), decided to take the idea one step further. He ordered all GAR members to visit their local cemeteries on May 30th to honor those who had given their lives in the war. He chose a day in late May to be sure that northern flowers would be in bloom.

In 1874, his order inspired Congress to enact a law. Because of that law—and the kindness of a little girl from Kalamazoo—we now observe a national holiday called Memorial Day on the last Monday in May.

After She Turned Twenty

Josephine May didn't get to see that law in action. She had died two years earlier from unknown causes and was buried at the Mountain Home cemetery in Kalamazoo.

Ella May lived a longer, fuller life. When she grew up, she married Joseph Willson and lived in Spokane, Washington, where she devoted much of her time to helping the poor in her community. When she died in 1901, her obituary noted that she was "brave, unselfish, and noble" and known for her patriotic spirit. For the part she played in helping establish Memorial Day, she was made an honorary member of the GAR. It is said that her body was wrapped in the American flag before she was put to rest, close to her sister and parents.

Sources

Center for Civil War Research, The. "Civil War Memory/ Memorial Day." Accessed April 7, 2013. www.civilwar-center.olemiss.edu/memorial_day.shtml.

Civil War Archive, The. "Michigan: 2nd Regiment Infantry." Accessed May 29. 2013. www.civilwararchive.com/ Unreghst/unmiinf1.htm#2nd.

"First to Decorate Soldiers' Graves." Unknown newspaper, unknown date, from the Western Michigan University Archives and Regional History Collections.

"Origin of Memorial Day." *The New York Times*, May 25, 1902.

ONE FINAL FACT

Poet Will Carleton remembered Ella May's efforts to honor the Civil War dead in the sixth stanza of his work titled "Cover Them Over."

Tricia McNaughton won seven out of nine matches in the first meet that she entered.

TRICIA MCNAUGHTON (SAUNDERS)

Wrestling with the Rules
(1966–)

In the 1970s, Tricia McNaughton had no choice but to wrestle against boys. The real surprise was how often she won.

Patricia "Tricia" McNaughton came from a family of wrestlers. Her grandfather was a nationally ranked wrestler at the University of Michigan, and her father and brothers enjoyed the sport, too. After sitting through dozens of their practices and **meets**, she announced to her family that she was bored with watching. At seven years old, she wanted to begin her own wrestling career.

"I'd roll around the carpet with my little brother, Andrew," Tricia told a *Sports Illustrated* reporter. Her parents didn't have the heart to tell her about the challenges she'd face in the male-dominated sport and neither did the Ann Arbor Wrestling Warriors Club, which made her its first female member.

In her first tournament, she won seven of nine **matches** against boys. At age nine, she became the first female to win a Michigan state title. By the time she was ten, she'd also earned a regional championship. Suddenly, she was in the spotlight: "Hundreds of people would crowd around the mat whenever I wrestled. TV crews followed me everywhere."

Not everyone approved of Tricia competing. Some opponents were coached to hurt her. And when she tried to enter a national tournament as the only female among 850 wrestlers, the people in charge wouldn't let her weigh in. Her parents sued the sponsors, and a judge sided with Tricia. But the decision came too late for her to join the event.

By age twelve, she had racked up a win-loss record of 181–23 against male competitors from across the country. That record would have been outstanding no matter what gender she was.

Tricia would have loved to compete for her high school, but she never got the chance. According to the statewide rules of the time, no girls could participate on boys' athletic school teams. Instead, she used her strong and limber body to excel in a different sport, one that *was* open to girls: gymnastics.

After graduating from Huron High School, she went on to college and earned a bachelor's degree in bacteriology, the study of one-celled organisms.

After She Turned Twenty

In 1988, a competitor she'd known since childhood urged Tricia to return to wrestling. Thanks to **Title IX**, the rules

After she stopped competing, Tricia (*kneeling, third from right*) went on to coach other women in her sport.

relating to female athletes had changed. Now they could compete in "men's sports" in high school and college. And, across the nation and the world, organizations began to host tournaments at which older female wrestlers could measure themselves against other women.

Tricia was among the first American women to take advantage of this opportunity. Training hard with the help of her husband, the Olympian Townsend Saunders, she was able to win the world championship in her **weight class** in her first year of competition. During her career, she did that three more times—the most of any American wrestler, male or female. She also won eleven national championships.

After she retired in 2001, Tricia became a strong advocate for women on the **governing board** for her sport. She also used her skills and knowledge to coach wrestlers at every level. She was honored for her work with these athletes by being named an American coach at the first-ever Olympic games to include women's wrestling, held in Athens, Greece, in 2004.

For all she achieved, it's not surprising that Tricia McNaughton Saunders was the first woman to be named to both the national and international halls of fame for her sport. After earning a second degree, she now serves as a **physician assistant** at a sports clinic in her adopted hometown of Phoenix, Arizona. She is also the mother of three children—all athletes like her, but they prefer soccer.

Sources

Finn, Mike. "Women's Wrestling's Reluctant Pioneers." *WIN Magazine*. Accessed October 9, 2013. www.win-magazine.com/current-past-issues/womens-wrestlings-reluctant-pioneers.

Lidz, Franz. "American Gladiator." *Sports Illustrated*, August 8, 1994.

National Wrestling Hall of Fame. "Tricia Saunders." Accessed October 8, 2013. nwhof.org/stillwater/hall-of-fame/#type=hof&honoree=1596.

Places to Visit

Tricia is honored with a plaque in the Michigan Women's Hall of Fame, 213 West Malcolm X Street, Lansing. For more information, see www.michiganwomenshalloffame. org or call 517–484–1880.

ONE FINAL FACT

As a child, Tricia was unbeatable nationwide in the fifty-pound weight class.

Though very young when they started out, the Supremes—Cindy Birdsong, Diana Ross (*center*), and Mary Wilson—often dressed in elegant gowns.

DIANA ROSS

A Supreme Songstress
(1944–)

*She wasn't the best singer at Motown Records. But she
had something many others didn't: star quality.*

Diane "Diana" Ross was the second of six children born to
Fred and Ernestine Ross of Detroit. Their first child, Barbara, was known in the family as the "pretty child." Diana,
who was bony and big-eyed, didn't have her sister's good
looks, but she didn't let that stop her from being the center
of attention. At age five, she appeared in a school play based
on the fairy tale of Hansel and Gretel. She was asked to hold
a flashlight in front of herself while she sang a song. Instead
she shone it on her own face, as if it were a spotlight.

Diana got her love of singing from her mother. Ernestine Ross had entered singing contests when she was young
and even considered a career in show business. Though she
set all that aside when she got married and started a family,

she still loved to sing gospel hymns in the house. Her voice was said to be sweet, lilting, and high-pitched.

At the age of eleven, Diana made friends with a neighborhood boy named William "Smokey" Robinson. Smokey was four years older and knew all the popular songs. He and his friends would stand on the street corner and sing them in harmony, snapping their fingers to keep the beat. This kind of singing was called "doo-wop," and Diana loved it.

With a nudge from Smokey, she began to practice her own talent by singing in front of a mirror in her bedroom. Her parents took note and even asked her to sing at a party they hosted for some friends. After wowing the crowd, she passed the hat. "I collected enough money to buy myself a pair of patent leather tap dance shoes," she remembered.

By the late 1950s, Diana's family had become so large that they needed to find a new place to live. Mr. Ross had heard about a newly built neighborhood of quality, affordable housing. The family moved to the Brewster-Douglass Housing Projects on Diana's fourteenth birthday.

At about this time, three young men had formed a singing group called the Primes. While the boys were good, their manager, Milton Jenkins, thought they could get twice as much attention if they performed with a group of young women. He told his girlfriend about the idea, and she told her sister, Florence Ballard, who liked to sing. Florence recruited her friend Mary Wilson, and the two girls, both teenagers from the Brewster Projects, set out to find at least one more to round out their group. Betty McGlown signed on.

Then one of the Primes had an idea. He'd heard a young girl singing with some friends on her front porch. Would the Primettes, as the trio of girls was known, consider adding a fourth voice? The answer was an excited yes! Diana was asked to join the group.

But Diana's father stood in the way. He was a strict disciplinarian, and he didn't like the idea of his teenage daughter being out late at night with who knows what kind of people. Mrs. Ross, who remembered her own long-ago dreams of being a singer, convinced him to let Diana go.

It didn't take many practices before the girls realized that they sounded great together. But who was going to be the lead singer? Being the first member *and* the singer with the strongest voice, Florence thought the role should be hers. But Diana challenged her. After a stare down and a cooling-off period, it was agreed that the newest member could sing lead *sometimes*.

Despite the tension in the group, the Primettes pulled together to compete in a talent show at the 1960 Detroit/Windsor Freedom Festival—and won.

The next month, they got even braver. Almost every singer in town was trying to get an invitation to **audition** at Motown, a hot new recording **studio**. Smokey Robinson was one of the first to get signed to a **contract**. Diana decided to use her friendship with the young man to get the Primettes in the door.

The four girls arrived in matching blouses, skirts, and scarves, looking confident but feeling very nervous. While their audition was going on, the owner of the company, Berry Gordy, walked in and out of the room, conducting other business. Florence gave it her all as the lead singer on most of the tunes, but what stopped Berry in his tracks was Diana's distinctive voice. It was untrained; in fact, he told her that she sang through her nose. But her voice had passion. So he sat the four girls down for a talk.

After he learned that Mary and Diana were sixteen, Florence was seventeen, and Betty was eighteen, he stopped the conversation and told them to come back after they had all graduated from high school. At first, they were terribly disappointed. Then they got angry and vowed that they would come back every day until he signed them.

By the end of the summer, Betty decided that she wanted to stop singing; she quit the group and was replaced by Barbara Martin.

In the fall, Berry Gordy signed his first female **solo** artist, but she needed some backup singers to work with. So he decided to give the Primettes a try. When the girls heard the news, they jumped up and down in the studio hallway, embracing and laughing. This was their big chance.

The recording session went well. Then they were asked to help out on a couple of other artists' songs.

In late 1960, the Primettes made two recordings of their own. Berry was so pleased with the quality that he offered them a recording contract with Motown. But there was a catch: they'd have to change their name.

The girls tried to think of ideas and talked to family and friends, then made a list of all the alternatives. It was Florence who finally picked the winner: the Supremes.

Diana couldn't wait to get home to share her good news. But her dad didn't see it that way. He wanted her to go to college and do something sensible with her life. He even refused to co-sign her paperwork. Again, her mother stepped in and, with a swipe of a pen, made sure that Diana could participate.

Before her career could take off, though, Diana had to graduate from high school. She attended Detroit's Cass Tech, a top-rated school with special classes in the arts and technology, where she focused on fashion design and joined the swim team. With her busy singing schedule, she struggled a bit with her grades. But she did earn her cap and gown with the rest of the class of 1962. She was even voted best-dressed.

In 1962, Barbara Martin dropped out of the Supremes. The remaining girls decided it would be better to move forward as a trio.

Two years of touring followed that decision. During that time, they improved their harmonies and learned how to dress, do their makeup, and style their hair. (Motown set high standards for appearance.) Berry Gordy also named Diana the lead singer, believing her voice had the best chance of **crossover** success.

In 1964, Diana Ross and the Supremes scored their first number-one hit with "Where Did Our Love Go?"

After She Turned Twenty

Between 1964 and 1967, the group produced nine more number-one singles, giving the Beatles some competition on the musical charts.

Love was a frequent theme in the Supremes' music; their song titles included "You Can't Hurry Love" and "Stop in the Name of Love." But there wasn't a lot of affection in the trio. After missing practices and performances, Florence Ballard was fired; Cindy Birdsong took her place. And there was grumbling about the fact that only one singer—Diana—got singled out for star treatment.

Berry thought the Supremes could stand on their own, so he encouraged Diana to step out as a solo act. But she worried about making the move. She'd spent nine years with the other girls, helping build their success. "Will I be okay?" she wondered in her autobiography. "Will my records be hits, too?" In 1970, she got her answer. Her debut album included tunes like "Reach Out and Touch Somebody's Hand" and "Ain't No Mountain High Enough." The second of these songs became her first solo number-one hit.

As it turned out, Diana recorded twenty-three more albums over the years and had great success as a solo singer. She also served as a **mentor** to another Motown sensation: the Jackson 5 and their lead singer, Michael Jackson. But she wanted to try other things to stretch herself as a performer. That led her to take on her first movie role as **jazz** singer Billie Holiday in *Lady Sings the Blues*.

Diana still performs in concert. She sings here in 2013 in Chile.

Though Diana's voice was different in tone from Billie's, the critics thought she did a great job. And her peers did, too; they nominated her for a best actress **Oscar**. An album made up of the songs she sang in the film sold nearly two million copies.

Diana followed up that performance with the starring role in *Mahogany*, a 1975 film about an aspiring fashion designer. Putting her high school training to good use, she even got to design the clothes she wore.

Her third movie, *The Wiz*, was a musical version of the Wizard of Oz story with an all-black cast. In it, she played Dorothy opposite her friend Michael Jackson as the scarecrow.

Diana even made it to Broadway, where a one-woman musical performance, *An Evening with Diana Ross*, earned her a special **Tony Award**.

During the 1970s, Diana also had a very full family life. She married and gave birth to three daughters. During her second marriage, begun in the 1980s, she welcomed two sons. For all the fame and fortune she found in her career, Diana has always considered her children to be her greatest accomplishment.

When she lived in Europe with her second husband, she built a whole new audience of fans on that continent. Her album *One Woman* sold more than four million copies—enough to be called "quadruple platinum."

Diana Ross continues to impress the world with her music; she is still touring in her seventies. And the honors for her body of work keep coming in. To name just a few, she has been inducted as a member of the Supremes into the Rock and Roll Hall of Fame (1988) and received a **Grammy** Lifetime Achievement Award. She was also recognized as a **Kennedy Center Honoree**.

In an interview, she shared this piece of advice for young girls who want to follow in her footsteps: "You can't just sit there and wait for people to give you that golden dream. You've got to get out there and make it happen for yourself."

Sources

Rock and Roll Hall of Fame and Museum, The. "The Supremes." Accessed August 8, 2013. www.rockhall.com/inductees/the-supremes.

Ross, Diana. *Secrets of a Sparrow*. New York: Random House, 1993.

Taraborrelli, J. Randy. *Diana Ross: A Biography*. New York: Citadel Press, 2007.

Whitall, Susan. "A Rare Interview with Singer Diana Ross." *The Detroit News*, April 13, 2007.

ONE FINAL FACT

Diana Ross has *two* stars on the Hollywood Walk of Fame: one with the Supremes and one by herself.

From the time that she was a small child, Anna Howard Shaw felt called to be a minister.

ANNA HOWARD SHAW

A Pint-Sized Pioneer
(1847–1919)

As a girl of twelve, Anna took the lead in helping
her fatherless family make a home in the
untamed forests of Michigan.

Have you ever had to leave your friends and make a new life in a strange place? Anna Howard Shaw did. She moved from one country to another and then from a city house to an unfinished cabin in the middle of the Michigan wilderness—all before she turned thirteen.

Anna was the sixth child of an English grain merchant and his wife. Mr. Shaw's profits rose and fell several times during the 1840s, and his family suffered through the changes. That made him decide to see if he could do better by working in America. When Anna was just two, he sailed there alone. More than two years passed before he could earn enough money to bring his large family over to join him.

The voyage across the Atlantic was frightening. Sailing from Liverpool, England, the Shaws lived through a storm that raged for days. Anna and her siblings were huddled belowdecks. "I was then little more than four years old, and the first vivid memory I have is that of being on [the ship] and having a mighty wave roll over me," she explained in her autobiography. "I was lying . . . under a hatchway, and the water poured from above, almost drowning me."

On the second day of the storm, the masts broke off the ship. On the third day, it sprung a leak. But, luckily, another ship came to the rescue and towed them to the nearest port.

The next time they tried to cross the ocean, it was much calmer, and the ship sailed quickly and easily to the port of New York City. Mr. Shaw was so happy to see his family that he brought gifts for the children. Anna was given a little saw and hatchet: "In the years ahead of me I was to use tools as well as my brothers did, as I proved when I helped to build our frontier home."

At first, the Shaws settled in Massachusetts, where Anna and her siblings went to school, met many of the leading citizens of the day, and were exposed to the **abolition movement**. One day, she even discovered an escaped slave hiding in the family cellar, but the woman hurried away to her next stop on the **Underground Railroad** before Anna could talk to her.

In 1858, when Anna was eleven, her father bought land in Michigan, 900 miles west of where they lived. Why so far away? Land was cheap in the new states in the middle of the country, and many people in the East felt they could make a better living by moving there to farm.

Unfortunately, Mr. Shaw bought land in the wrong part of the state. His acreage, in Mecosta County, wasn't farmland; it was forested. But that didn't stop him and his oldest son, James, from clearing a space among the trees and using the timber to put up a basic cabin.

Mr. Shaw then returned to Massachusetts, leaving his son behind to establish ownership of the land. A few months later, Mrs. Shaw, her three daughters, and a young son of eight joined James in the Michigan wilderness. Mr. Shaw stayed back East with two of the couple's other sons.

The journey to their new home in the country was as challenging as their ocean voyage. At that time, in 1859, the train tracks only extended as far as Grand Rapids. That forced the family to travel the last hundred miles by wagon through a thick forest. Almost every available inch of space in the wagon was filled with bedding, clothing, and food. There was so little room to ride that the children took turns walking.

Along the way, they had to cross many streams. The wheels of the heavy wagon sometimes sank into the streambeds, and the only way to free them was to empty everything that was stored in the wagon. Fallen trees lay across their path, and—with no signs to guide the Shaws—they lost their way many times. At one point, a box of piglets broke open, and the whole family raced to round them up in the dark woods.

On the last day of their journey, their hearts were light as they looked forward to seeing their new home. But when they reached the clearing, their faces fell. What they found wasn't a completed, comfortable cabin; it was just four walls and a roof. Doors and windows were simply squares cut into the timbers. There was no floor *and* no furniture to be seen.

For Mrs. Shaw, who had dutifully followed her husband to America and then helped him establish himself in Massachusetts, this primitive structure in the wilderness was just too much to bear. She sank to the ground and buried her head in her hands.

The children were frightened to see their mother so sad. Their first night, sleeping on pine branches spread across the cabin's dirt floor, was quiet and tense. Bonfires outside kept the wild animals of the woods at bay.

The next day, the Shaws held a family council. Though she was only twelve, Anna took an active role in the discussion. "The division of labor was that mother should do our sewing, and my older sisters the housework," she explained in her autobiography. "My brothers and I were to do the work out of doors. . . . the first thing [we did] was to put doors and windows into the yawning holes father had left for them, and to lay a board flooring over the earth inside our cabin walls, and these duties we accomplished before we had occupied our new home [for two weeks]."

Brother James, whom Anna called "our tower of strength," made basic furniture to fill their new home. He also built a strong friendship with the Indians who passed by them on a regular basis; however, a couple of months after the family arrived, James fell ill and was forced to travel East for an operation. "He was never able to return to us," Anna noted sadly.

In his absence, Anna and Harry fed the family—spearing fish in the creek and gathering wild fruits in the forest—and started to clear their plot of land. Anna, who'd gotten plenty of practice with her toy saw and hatchet, soon became an expert at cutting down trees.

When winter came, the nearby creek froze over. To make sure that the family didn't have to go through another season of melting snow to make water, Anna decided to dig a well as soon as the weather turned. Her little brother was too small to help, leaving the work to his sister with assistance from a neighbor who lived almost twenty miles away. The digging was difficult work. After the hole was deep enough, it also had to be lined with slabs of wood to keep the water clean. Anna recalled: "It was not a thing of beauty, but it was a thoroughly practical well, and it remained the only one we had during the twelve years the family occupied the cabin."

In the spring, she also figured out a way to tap maple trees for their sap, and the two children carried home what they had gathered in pails slung from wooden frames they wore over their shoulders. That first year, she proudly noted, "we made one hundred and fifty pounds of sugar and a barrel of syrup." In the summer, Anna and Harry tended the potatoes and corn they had planted among the stumps of their acreage.

After eighteen months of living in the Michigan wilderness, the family was once again joined by Mr. Shaw. He brought with him a box of books, which Anna eagerly tore open "as a starving man falls upon food." (Anna had tried attending a country school three miles from her home, but she knew more than the teacher.)

The books were also the source of her first rebellion against her parents. After spending a rare day reading in the woods, she returned to find an angry father. He accused her of being idle while the family needed her to work in the home. And he predicted that, if she continued in this way, she would never amount to anything.

Anna was stung by the criticism; she knew how hard she had worked in the months he had been gone, *and* she knew that she would have a career. Though she was only fourteen, she had already felt her **calling** to preach. Anna quietly explained to her father that the books were important to her future, because "someday I am going to college."

Her dream was postponed by the start of the **Civil War**. As soon as President Abraham Lincoln called for troops to save the Union, two of Anna's brothers and her father signed up to serve. Anna was left in charge.

At age fifteen, she began to teach school, and every bit of her six-dollar-a-week salary went into keeping the family afloat. The war drove up the prices of everyday items like sugar and coffee, so money was tight. To get by, the Shaws took in boarders and made quilts. Young Harry did what he could to harvest the crops and keep the livestock healthy.

During this period, one of Anna's older sisters died in childbirth, and the other moved into Big Rapids. It was a lonely and frightening time at the Shaw cabin, but Anna's dream of college still burned bright.

When the war ended in 1865 and her father and brothers returned home, Anna was freed from her family responsibilities. Though she could now set aside more of her teaching salary to pay for college, the fund was slow to build up. She vowed to find a trade that would pay her more.

Before long, she quit teaching and moved to Big Rapids where there were more jobs available. Accustomed to hard work, she hoped to take on a physical job, but the construction trades weren't open to women at that time. She finally settled upon sewing to make ends meet.

Within a month of finding a position, though, something happened that dramatically changed her plans. Mariana Thompson, a famous female minister, came to town to speak. Anna was the first person to file into the church to listen. Spellbound by the woman's **sermon**, Anna was also the last to leave. She then approached the woman and poured out her life story, including her own desire to preach. The minister's words to her were simple and direct. "My child," she said, "give up your foolish idea of learning a trade, and go to school. You can't do anything until you have an education."

Anna wasted no time in putting that advice to good use. Despite being older than her peers, she began to attend the local high school. The principal, also a woman, learned about Anna's career plans and put her in all of the school's speaking and debating classes. "I was given every opportunity to hold forth to helpless classmates when the spirit of eloquence moved me," Anna said.

During an evening program to which parents and friends were invited, Anna rose to speak. Overcome by the size of the audience, she fainted. Sympathetic friends carried her into a nearby room and revived her. After a few minutes of rest, she took the stage again, this time making it to the end of her remarks. The audience then let out a cheer for the brave girl who didn't give up.

After all the hardships she had faced since moving to Michigan, Anna was not going to let a little stage fright set her back.

After She Turned Twenty

As Anna's talent for speaking grew, the principal arranged for her to meet a Methodist **elder** from the area. Over coffee and cookies, the man asked Anna if she'd like to preach before a meeting of elders in Osceola County. At first, she thought she wasn't ready for such an honor; after all, though she was in her twenties, she was still in high school. But after praying for guidance, she accepted the invitation. The sermon was a success and inspired the man to ask if she'd go with him as he traveled to other places in mid-Michigan. At the end of their tour together, she was given a license to preach.

Though her family, believing the ministry was for men only, did not approve of her calling, Anna continued her

After earning degrees in theology and medicine, Anna went on to serve as a national leader in the women's suffrage movement.

quest. In the fall of 1873, at the age of twenty-five, she entered Albion College with plans to earn a degree.

She grew as a student and as a person during her time at Albion. But she also felt that she had to catch up with her peers. As a result, she left Albion after only two years and moved on to study **theology** at Boston University in Massachusetts. She was the only woman in her class of forty-three ministers in training.

Anna had to deal with discrimination in Boston. For instance, she did not receive a free room like the male students did, and she sometimes had to live for weeks at a time on just milk and crackers. In spite of this, she became the first woman in America to be **ordained** a minister in the Methodist faith. But that was not the end of her accomplishments.

In 1886 she earned a medical degree from the same university. She also became involved in the temperance movement, which tried to discourage Americans from drinking, but it was when she joined the fight to guarantee women's suffrage—the right to vote—that she became known across the country. Anna was a great friend of Susan B. Anthony, one of the leaders of the suffrage movement. And when Susan became too old to lead their organization, Anna stepped in and served as president for eleven years.

When the United States entered World War I, Anna was chosen to lead the Woman's Committee of the Council of National Defense. Her assignment was to organize women's work on the **home front**. For her efforts, she was awarded the Distinguished Service Medal, the highest military honor that a civilian can receive.

Anna Howard Shaw continued to lecture for women's rights for the remaining years of her life. She died in 1919, one year before the suffrage **amendment** became law.

Sources

Franzen, Trisha. *Anna Howard Shaw: The Work of Woman Suffrage*. Champaign: University of Illinois Press, 2014.

Shaw, Anna Howard. *The Story of a Pioneer*. Cleveland: The Pilgrim Press, 1994.

"Dr. Anna H. Shaw, Suffragist, Dies." *The New York Times*, July 2, 1919.

Places to Visit

Anna is honored with a plaque in the Michigan Women's Hall of Fame, 213 West Malcolm X Street, Lansing. For more information, see www.michiganwomenshalloffame. org or call 517–484–1880.

A statue of Anna may be found in a park at 426 South Michigan Avenue in Big Rapids, and she is the subject of a state of Michigan historical marker on 22 Mile Road east of US 131 in Mecosta County.

ONE FINAL FACT

When Anna was a young girl, she practiced giving sermons by standing in the forest and talking to the trees.

Serena Williams (*right*) and sister Venus hug their father, Richard, at one of the Compton, California, tennis courts where they learned to play.

SERENA WILLIAMS

Queen of the Court
(1981–)

*With practice and perseverance, a toddler
with a tennis racquet grew up to be the
number-one player in the world.*

Picture a little girl, just three years old, wearing a white skirt printed with pink, gray, and purple flowers. Her hair is braided and tied together on top of her head. In her hand is an adult-sized tennis racquet, and across the net is her father softly tossing balls for her to hit. "Good job, Serena," he says every time she connects. "Way to go."

That was the scene the first time that Serena Jameka Williams ever played tennis.

Born in her mother's Michigan hometown of Saginaw, Serena and her family soon moved to Compton, California, a suburb of Los Angeles. Compton was a tough town to grow up in, with gangs and violence just outside the door. Richard and Oracene Williams protected their five daughters by making sure that someone was always home with them. They also introduced them to tennis. Why tennis? One day Mr. Williams was watching a match on television and heard the announcer say that one of the female players made $40,000 for playing in a tournament. That was more than he made in a year. He vowed then and there to turn at least one of his daughters into a tennis superstar.

The tennis courts in Compton were not well kept up. There was broken glass. Cracks had formed in the concrete. And some courts didn't have nets. But they were a good enough place to learn the basics. The Williams family visited them frequently.

They would all pile into a van with a shopping cart full of balls. Some of those balls were fresh, right out of the can; when you hit them, they would zip across the net. Other balls were old and flat. The girls hated to hit those because they just wouldn't bounce. But their dad made them play with them anyway. "At Wimbledon," he'd say, "the balls will bounce low, just like these, so you have to be ready." (He was right; the courts at Wimbledon, the site of one of tennis's four **Grand Slam** events, are covered with grass, which makes tennis balls skid and stay close to the ground.)

At first, the Williamses would just play for fun and exercise. Then, when two of the girls—Venus at age six and Serena at five—showed real talent for the game, their parents started to play harder and pushed *them* to play harder. Soon the girls were practicing three or four hours a day, seven days a week. "My dad had us thinking, breathing, living tennis," Serena said in her autobiography.

Mr. Williams was also following the local tennis scene, looking for events that Venus and Serena could participate in to improve their skills. Once he got them into a **clinic** where tennis great Billie Jean King was playing. "It was a big, big day for us," said Serena. "I remember going through our closet, trying to pick out just the right outfit to wear." At the court, Billie Jean walked over to the girls to introduce herself and then hit them some balls. Because Serena was nervous, she didn't hit them back very well. And she cried when her sister did better. But Serena still called the experience "pretty huge."

The family also attended professional tournaments from time to time. Serena was very impressed by a player named Gabriela Sabatini. Big, broad-shouldered, and strong, Gabriela didn't look like the other girls on the tour. These were traits that Serena, then a tiny little thing, wished she could have.

It wasn't long after that Serena started playing in local tennis leagues and developing a strong game, if not yet strong muscles.

At this time, her older sister Venus began to draw national attention. Tennis coaches from out of state visited the family in Compton and encouraged the Williamses to send their daughter away so that she could get better coaching. Up to this point, their parents had been the only coaches the girls had ever had. The couple decided that

Venus could take this step but only if Serena was included, too.

The family moved to central Florida to enroll the two girls in a rigorous tennis program. But school was still in the picture. Venus and Serena went to class until one in the afternoon, then practiced their tennis skills until suppertime. Within a year, Serena had worked her way up to a 46–3 record and was ranked number one among players under ten years of age nationwide.

The natural next step in Venus and Serena's development as players would have been the junior tournament circuit for players ten to eighteen. But their parents said no. They wanted the girls to lead normal lives. They didn't want them to be traveling around for long periods of time, missing school and their other interests: ballet, gymnastics, and karate.

Instead, Venus and Serena stayed put in Florida and played against even stronger opponents: boys. Boys played a faster, harder game, and they taught the Williams girls how to compete like that, too.

In 1995, Serena took part in her first professional tournament. It was a bad day for her. The score—6–1, 6–1—wasn't even close. Yet Serena felt her opponent wasn't that good. So what held her back from winning? "I think the moment was a little too big for my fourteen-year-old self," she explained. "It messed with my head to be playing in front of a great, big crowd, underneath these great, big expectations." She realized that she wasn't yet mature enough to succeed on the circuit, so she took two years off before competing as a pro again.

In 1997, Serena tried her luck at another tournament and was easily defeated in the first round of the women's singles bracket. But she and her sister paired up for the doubles competition and made it all the way to the semifinals. That was a victory in their eyes.

The next year, Venus and Serena paired up again in a tournament and ending up winning it. "I went from being a little overwhelmed and out of place to believing I was untouchable, unstoppable," Serena said. She finished 1997 as the ninety-ninth best female tennis player in the world.

When Serena turned sixteen, she experienced a growth spurt that gave her game new power. Suddenly, she could hit the ball *hard,* and her serve became her favorite weapon.

Also, when she was sixteen, her dad negotiated her first **endorsement deal**. It was with a European sportswear company named Puma. Serena was excited; she loved clothes and was always putting together fun outfits from the big closet she shared with her sisters. With Puma, she got to help design her own tennis clothes. Together they came up with some outrageous ideas using bold colors and unusual fabrics. Breaking out of the traditional tennis skirt-and-shirt mode, she once wore a formfitting, one-piece outfit to a tournament. "People started to wonder what I'd wear next," she said.

After the girls graduated from high school, Venus took art classes at a local college whenever she had time off from the professional tennis circuit. She tried to talk her younger sister into joining her, but Serena enjoyed the break from school too much. Serena explained: "I was just interested in watching television, hanging out, and playing tennis." Venus lost her patience with Serena and signed her up for classes anyway. Serena was glad that she did: "School was a blast! I studied design and fashion, so most of my courses had me sewing and drawing, learning the construction of a garment, considering which fabric might work on which design." Those classes made her think about fashion as a career—if her tennis game didn't work out, that is.

In 1998, Serena started off slow and finished strong. For the first time, she had to face her sister in a match, which Venus won. Serena also lost to several other top-ten rivals. But by midyear, she started to see great improvement in her game. Playing with Max Mirnyi in **mixed doubles**, she won at Wimbledon and the U.S. Open—half of the Grand Slam events in the tennis year. She also added to her singles record, finishing the year ranked at number twenty.

In 1999, Serena started the season even more determined to succeed. With her sister as her partner, she won the doubles title at the French Open. At the U.S. Open, she won both the doubles *and* singles titles. With three more Grand Slam titles to her name, her year-end ranking rose to number four. She achieved all this in just her second full year on the professional circuit.

In 2000, Serena suffered an injury that set her progress back a bit, but she still ended up winning another doubles title at Wimbledon with Venus. The two also teamed up to win a gold medal at the Olympics in September. Was there anything better than winning for your country, Serena wondered?

Six months later, however, a new challenge faced the Williamses. Because of a knee injury, Venus withdrew from a California tournament right before a semifinal match with her sister. So Serena got an automatic win. Those who came to see the girls battle it out were upset; some even accused Venus of faking her injury, so that Serena—the less experienced player—could get to the finals. When Serena entered the stadium for the final match, there were boos. Some people even shouted racial slurs at her. During the entire match, the crowd cheered for her opponent, a Belgian woman—something rarely seen at an American tournament when an American is playing. Serena got rattled: "I couldn't get into any kind of rhythm. I couldn't focus or get anything going." During one of the rest periods, she sat down and cried into her towel.

Then something inside her changed. She thought about Althea Gibson, the first black person to play professional tennis, who faced discrimination everywhere she went. And Serena decided right then and there that she had to keep playing, and she had to win.

After **double faulting** at the start, Serena began to win point after point. Slowly, the crowd came over to her side. An unknown voice stood out above the rest: "Come on, Serena. You can do it." And she did. She ended up winning the match 4–6, 6–4, 6–2 and afterward nearly collapsed with relief.

At a press conference later, 19-year-old Serena thanked her father, her sister, and the few people who cheered for her throughout the match. "And to those of you who didn't," she said, "I love you anyway."

After She Turned Twenty

The next few years were amazing for Serena Williams. She won four Grand Slam singles titles in seven months (three in 2002 and the Australian Open in 2003)—just the fifth woman to hold them all at the same time. She also rose to become the number-one female player in the world.

But that rapid rise was followed by a fast fall. A knee surgery put her out of action for eight weeks. Then the unthinkable happened. Her oldest sister, Yetunde, was killed in a shooting in their California hometown.

Serena took time off to recover from this terrible loss. But it wasn't enough. She became too depressed to return to her sport. She wouldn't leave her apartment. She also stopped talking to the people she loved. After several weeks of getting the silent treatment, her sisters flew in to see what was the matter. They made her promise to see a **therapist**. For a while, she went every day.

What Serena learned from this experience was that she had focused too much on making other people happy: her parents, her sponsors, her fans. If she was going to return to tennis, it had to be because *she* wanted to, not because others expected her to.

Serena finishes a powerful serve while competing in the Wimbledon
Championships in England in 2014.

A trip to West Africa helped her make a decision. When she visited the places where her ancestors had been captured and held before being forced onto slave ships, she began to cry. How terrible it must have been for them, she thought. And how amazing that any were able to survive. She came away thinking she was part of the strongest race in human history: "We will not be denied. I will not be denied. I can do anything."

Because she'd been away for months from the tour, her ranking had dropped to 139th in the world. To get back into shape, she started to play some smaller tournaments. She got beaten badly. Her sportswear sponsor hinted that the company might drop her if she didn't start winning again. And the news media were unkind to her, too, focusing on how much weight she'd gained. But Serena didn't let any of that affect her. Instead, she used it to motivate herself to work even harder.

When she got to the Australian Open in 2007, she felt ready to compete again at the highest level. And she did, defeating six high-ranking players before winning in the finals.

The next year, Serena and Venus again played for the U.S. in the Olympics. And again they took a gold medal as doubles partners. With her final stroke of the competition, she also regained the number-one ranking in the world. It had been five years and one month since she was last in that spot.

In 2014, Serena Williams turned thirty-three *and* marked her thirtieth year as a tennis player. Despite a serious health condition (she had a blood clot removed from her lung in 2011), she is still going strong. Throughout her career, she has won 56 singles championships, 22 doubles championships, and four Olympic gold medals (including doubles *and* singles medals in 2012). She is also the leading money-winner among female athletes.

Wanting to use that money for a good cause, she started the Serena Williams Foundation. The foundation has two purposes: to support American children who have been the victims of violence and to build schools in Africa for children who couldn't otherwise afford an education.

Sources

Battersby, Kate. "Stunning Serena Wins Fifth Wimbledon Singles Title." Wimbledon. Accessed May 8, 2013. www.wimbledon.com/en_GB/news/articles/2012-07-07/201207071341671882794.html.

Wertheim, Jon. "Focused Serena Dominant in Gold Medal Win Over Sharapova." *Sports Illustrated*. Accessed May 8, 2013. sportsillustrated.cnn.com/2012/olympics/2012/writers/jon_wertheim/08/04/serena-williams-gold-domination.

Williams, Serena, and Daniel Paisner. *Serena Williams: On the Line*. New York: Grand Central Publishing, 2009.

Williams, Venus, Serena Williams, and Hillary Beard. *Venus & Serena: Serving from the Hip*. Boston: HMH Books for Young Readers, 2005.

Places to Visit

Serena is honored with a plaque in the Michigan Women's Hall of Fame, 213 West Malcolm X Street, Lansing. For more information, see www.michiganwomenshalloffame. org or call 517–484–1880.

ONE FINAL FACT

In 2004, Serena launched her own fashion line. She calls it *Aneres*—her first name spelled backward.

GLOSSARY

4-H—A U.S. government program that helps young people in rural areas learn about farming as well as other useful skills such as carpentry and home economics.

abolitionist—A person who fought to free blacks from slavery. The **abolition movement** lasted from the 1830s until the Thirteenth Amendment to the U.S. Constitution—making slavery illegal—was ratified in 1865.

accompanist—One who plays music for a singer or dancer.

activist—A person who believes strongly in a cause and takes action to benefit it.

agent—One who helps performers schedule their work and get paid for it.

amendment—An addition to a state or federal constitution.

ancestral home—The place where one's ancestors are buried.

artist-in-residence—An artistic professional who is invited by a college, museum, or arts organization to visit for a short time and share their skill with students.

audition—A test at which a performer is asked to demonstrate his or her talent.

bandanna—A colorful cotton scarf worn on the head or around the neck.

barge—A low-walled, flat-bottomed vessel that transports cargo.

batting practice—When someone pitches to a batter so he or she can warm up before a game.

bit part—A small part in a movie that may offer only one speaking line.

breeze—To run a racehorse at a medium speed for a short distance.

Broadway—A street in New York City on which many famous theaters can be found. Plays that find success here are often sent on tour around the country.

calling—A career that people feel very strongly drawn to.

chaplain—A member of the clergy who serves in the military.

choreographer—A person who develops dance steps for others to follow.

Civil War—A defining conflict in American history, fought from 1861 to 1865 between the United States (the Union) and Confederate states that chose to break away and form their own government.

classical music—A style of music that uses traditional orchestra instruments and is meant to be played as written. Its roots are in nineteenth-century Europe.

clergy—Leaders of religious congregations. Titles can include imam, minister, priest, or rabbi.

clinic—In sports, a workshop run by professional players who share tips to improve an amateur athlete's performance.

commercial license—A document that allows a pilot with 250 hours of flight time to be paid for his or her work.

Confederacy—A government formed in 1861 by southern states that withdrew from the United States. A **Confederate** was a soldier or sailor who fought for the Southern side in the Civil War.

contract—An agreement between laborers and management that specifies wages, benefits, and working conditions. In the movie and music industries, a contract ties a performer to a single studio.

Cooperstown—The city in New York where the Baseball Hall of Fame is located.

coveralls—A loose-fitting, one-piece work garment worn over clothing to protect it from damage.

cross-country flight—A pilot takes off from one airport and lands at another. In a **dual flight**, two pilots are on board.

crossover—A singer who fits into several categories of music and has broad appeal.

descend—To lower oneself.

desert—To leave the military without permission and with no plans of returning.

double fault—When a player tries to serve a tennis ball and steps twice over the baseline.

elder—A person in a congregation who helps a member of the clergy manage his or her church.

Emmy Award—The highest honor in the television industry.

endorsement deal—An agreement that gives money and equipment to an athlete in exchange for the use of his or her name and image.

enlist—To volunteer to fight in the military.

Equal Rights Amendment—A suggested amendment to the U.S. Constitution guaranteeing equal rights for women and men.

flow'ret—A poetic word for "flower."

Fugitive Slave Act of 1850—An act of Congress that provided Southern slaveholders with legal approval to capture slaves who had escaped to the North.

gale—A storm with 30- to 60-mile-per-hour winds.

Genius Grants—Cash awards given by the John D. and Catherine T. MacArthur Foundation to help creative people in their work.

governing board—A group of experts who sets the rules for a sport or other organization.

Grammy Award—The highest honor in the music industry.

Grand Army of the Republic—An organization of men who had served with the Union in the Civil War.

Grand Slam—The top four tennis tournaments in the world: Wimbledon (England), the French Open, the Australian Open, and the U.S. Open.

Great Depression—A time during the 1930s when economic problems led to a quarter of the American population losing their jobs and being unable to find work.

Hispanic—A person who has roots in Spain or a Spanish-speaking country.

home front—The people at home and their activities when the military is elsewhere fighting a war.

hot-walkers—Stable helpers who walk racehorses to cool them off after they have been exercised.

improvise—To make up something on the spur of the moment during a live performance.

infield—The diamond-shaped area of a baseball field that includes all the bases.

jazz—A free-spirited, American style of music allowing for improvisation that dates from the early twentieth century.

jockey—A person who rides horses professionally in races. An **apprentice jockey** has less than one year of experience and has won fewer than 40 races.

Kennedy Center Honors—Awards given by the John F. Kennedy Center for the Performing Arts to performers who have contributed significantly to American culture over a lifetime.

laborers—People who do manual labor or work for hourly wages at a business.

major leagues—The highest level of competition for professional baseball players.

management—The people, such as the president and vice presidents, who lead a business.

master class—A small class for advanced students taught by an older, more skilled person.

mentor—A wise and trusted advisor.

Métis—The child of an American Indian parent and a white parent, especially one who has French roots.

migrant worker—One who moves from farm to farm to plant, weed, or pick crops for money.

minimum wage—The least amount of wages that a business can pay by law for work that laborers have performed.

minor—A person under the age of 18.

minor leagues—Lower-tier baseball organizations that enable good players to develop their skills.

mixed doubles—In tennis, a team that is made up of a man and a woman.

modern dance—A free, expressive style of dancing started in the early twentieth century as a reaction to classical ballet.

mustered in—To be formally accepted for military service. To be **mustered out** is to be allowed to leave that service.

negotiate—To talk about the terms of a hoped-for agreement.

Negro Leagues—Major-league baseball organizations made up of black players who were excluded from the white leagues. They operated from 1887 until about 1960.

Ninety-Nines—A group founded in 1929 to support female pilots. There were 99 original members.

ordained—To be formally welcomed into a religion as a member of its clergy.

Oscar—The highest honor in the movie industry. The proper name is the Academy Award.

pesticides—Chemicals used to kill pests, such as destructive insects.

physician assistant—A person trained to provide medical services in partnership with a doctor.

picket—To stand outside a business and try to stop workers and customers from entering it during a strike.

plantation—A large farm, usually in a warm climate, that is worked by laborers who live on the land. Before the Civil War, American plantations were worked by enslaved blacks.

play-off—An athletic contest that has several rounds of competition.

post-traumatic stress disorder—An anxious feeling triggered by experiencing or witnessing a terrifying event.

punt—A small, shallow boat with a flat bottom and square ends.

quarter horse—An American horse breed that excels at running short distances of a quarter mile or less.

receptionist—An office worker who greets visitors, answers phones, and makes appointments, among other duties.

regiment—A small army with a special purpose within a larger army. For example, an infantry regiment (soldiers on foot) or a cavalry regiment (soldiers on horseback).

repose—To rest upon.

salvage—To remove a sunken ship or its cargo from water. A person who does this work is called a **salver**.

screen test—A filmed audition to see how an actor or actress might look and sound in a movie.

sermon—An inspirational speech given by a member of the clergy during a service.

Shipmasters Association—An international organization made up of ship captains.

sit-down strike—When workers occupy their place of employment and refuse to move until a strike is settled.

slave market—In nineteenth-century America, a place where black men, women, and children were held against their will until they were sold as slaves to the highest bidder.

soap opera—A radio or television program, often aired in the daytime, that tells the story of a group of characters in an overly dramatic way.

Social Security—A U.S. government program that provides financial assistance to the elderly and the disabled.

solo—To undertake by oneself.

sounding—A way of measuring the depth of an area of water using a lead weight and line.

squadron—In aviation, a group of pilots brought together for a special purpose.

steamship—A vessel with a steam-driven, coal-burning engine.

studio—A special space in which creative people practice their art.

Suzuki method—A way of teaching music to children that involves small steps and child-sized instruments.

test pilot—One who tries out new aircraft to make sure they fly as designed.

theology—The study of religious faith, practice, and experience.

therapist—One who is trained to help people overcome psychological problems.

thoroughbred—A breed of horse with European and Asian bloodlines that is best known for long-distance racing.

Title IX—A clause in a 1972 federal law that made gender discrimination in education (including sports) illegal for schools that receive federal aid.

Tony Award—The highest honor in the theater industry. The proper name is the Antoinette Perry Award.

transport license—A document that allows a pilot to fly the largest airplanes. He or she must have 1,500 hours of experience to qualify.

Triple Crown—The top three thoroughbred horse races in the U.S.: the Kentucky Derby, the Preakness Stakes, and the Belmont Stakes.

troupe—A group of dancers who travel around putting on shows.

tryout—A test of skills that an athlete has to pass before he or she may be accepted onto a team.

Underground Railroad—A system of secret routes and safe places for enslaved people to rest as they made their way north to freedom.

union—An organization of workers who gather together for a common purpose, such as negotiating contracts with their employers.

Union—The northern side during the Civil War, made up of 20 free states and five slave states that didn't join the Confederacy.

verdure—A lush, green landscape.

veterans' benefits—Payments from the federal government to former servicemen and women to cover medical services and other needs.

wake—A "track" of waves left by a ship as it moves through the water.

weight class—A way to pair up wrestlers for competition so that neither has an unfair advantage.

women's rights—Legal, political, and social rights for women that are equal to those of men.

World War II—A global conflict, which lasted from 1939 to 1945, between the Allies (led by Great Britain, the Soviet Union, and the U.S.) and the Axis countries (led by Germany and Japan).

wrestling match—When two wrestlers square off to see who will win. A **wrestling meet** is when groups of wrestlers compete.

PHOTO CREDITS

Grateful acknowledgment is made to the following individuals and institutions for their permission to include the photos in this book:

Fannie Baker: © istockphoto.com/duncan1890.

Betty Bloomer (Ford): Gerald R. Ford Presidential Library.

Dorothy Butler: Western Michigan University Archives and Regional History Collections.

Regina Carter: (*young*) Regina Carter; (*adult*) Susan Tusa/KRT/Newscom.

Sarah Emma Edmonds (Seelye): Bentley Historical Library, University of Michigan.

Nancy Harkness (Love): (*cover*) The Woman's Collection, Texas Woman's University, Denton, Texas; (*young*) National Aviation Hall of Fame; (*adult*) AP Images.

Julie Harris: (*young*) Digital Press Photos/Newscom; (*adult*) Columbia Pictures Corporation/Album/Newscom.

Marylou Hernandez (Olivarez-Mason): Marylou Olivarez-Mason.

Geraldine Hoff (Doyle): (*young*) Stephanie Doyle Gregg; (*"We Can Do It!" poster*) Smithsonian National Museum of American History.

Marilyn Jenkins: (*young*) Grand Rapids History & Special Collections Archives, Grand Rapids Public Library, Grand Rapids, Michigan; (*adult*) Grand Valley State University | Amanda Pitts.

Jane Johnston (Schoolcraft): Bentley Historical Library, University of Michigan.

Myra Komaroff (Wolfgang): Walter P. Reuther Library, Archives of Labor and Urban Affairs, Wayne State University.

Julie Krone: (*young*) Julie Krone, photo by Don Krone; (*adult*) Julian Herbert/ZUMA Press/Newscom.

Joan Leslie (Caldwell): (*young*) RKO/Album/Newscom; (*adult*) Byron Purvis/AdMedia/Newscom.

Maebelle Mason (Connell): Bentley Historical Library, University of Michigan.

Ella May (Willson): © istockphoto.com/JonnyJim.

Tricia McNaughton (Saunders): (*young*) MLive.com/Landov Media; (*adult*) Tony Rotundo/WrestlersAreWarriors.com.

Diana Ross: (*young*) LA Media Collection/Sunshine/ZUMA Press/Newscom; (*adult*) Felipe Trueba/EPA/Newscom.

Anna Howard Shaw: (*young*) Albion College Archives and Special Collections; (*adult*) Library of Congress, Prints & Photographs Division, photograph by Harris & Ewing, reproduction number LC-DIG-hec-05374.

Serena Williams: (*young*) Paul Harris, Pacific Coast News/Newscom; (*adult*) Michael Mayhew/Sportsphoto/Photoshot/Newscom.